CREATING CARING COMMUNITIES
with Books Kids Love

Nancy A. Chicola and **Eleanor B. English**

D1310374

Fulcrum Publishing
Golden, Colorado

We would like to dedicate this book to the future generation
of our families, Kristene Jordan and Hannah Wastyk,
as well as Joseph English IV and Jackson English.
May they always continue learning to care.

Text and interior photographs and illustrations
copyright © 2002 Nancy A. Chicola and Eleanor B. English

Library of Congress Cataloging-in-Publication Data
Chicola, Nancy A.
Creating caring communities with books kids love / Nancy A. Chicola
and Eleanor B. English.
    p. cm.
Includes bibliographical references and index.
ISBN 1-55591-919-7 (pbk.)
1. Affective education. 2. Caring—Study and teaching (Elementary)
3. Citizenship—Study and teaching (Elementary) 4. Children—Books and
reading. I. English, Eleanor B. II. Title.
LB1072 .C55 2002
970.15'3—dc21
                    2002008410

Printed in Canada
0 9 8 7 6 5 4 3 2 1

Book design: Patty Maher
Cover image: © 1998 Artville, Laura DeSantis illustrator

Fulcrum Publishing
16100 Table Mountain Parkway, Suite 300
Golden, Colorado 80403
(800) 992-2908 • (303) 277-1623
www.fulcrum-resources.com

Contents

Chapter 6—Our World

List of Photos

List of Reproducibles

Acknowledgments

This endeavor required the support from many people who gave freely of their time and expertise. We express our appreciation to these individuals:

SUNY at Buffalo State students at Professional Development Sites who piloted many of the activities in their field experiences at Big Tree Elementary in the Frontier Schools and in the Salamanca City Central Schools at both Prospect and Seneca Elementary Schools.

Betsy Budzinski and the second grade students at Boardmanville Elementary school, Cherie Whitcher's first-grade students at Prospect Elementary, and students from a variety of grade levels at the Native American Magnet School in Buffalo who participated in some of the activities and served as models for the photographs.

Photographers Richard Gates and William Sunderlin III as well as artist Richard Turner who created the artistic images that so aptly depicted the activities.

Shelia Boston for her musical expertise in writing the very relevant song, *Our Flag*, for primary children.

St. Bonaventure University's and Buffalo State's library staff, especially Ann Tenglund, for their support and aid in locating pertinent literature.

Introduction

Caring, the value that most Americans seem to agree is most necessary in adult life,
is rooted in the social and emotional development of childhood.
—Elias

Caring is a pebble that when thrown into a pond spreads influential rings to the family, school, community, and beyond. Teachers and parents must build a caring community in the classroom and at home to begin and carry on the task to help combat the lack of concern about and the proliferation of violence apparent in the world. Recently, there has been a strong focus on these problems in society. It is preferable to focus on prevention and long-term solutions rather than quick-fix reactions to violent acts. Certainly if violent behavior is learned, then young children are capable of learning caring behaviors as well. Attitudes and dispositions are formed early in life, therefore, the school plays an important role in teaching children to behave humanely and compassionately.

A caring curriculum is longitudinal, beginning in childhood and developing throughout the early and middle grades. Although a curriculum includes content knowledge and skills, for caring to be fostered and developed the emphasis should also be placed on perspectives that include attitudes, feelings, and dispositions. Observable indicators of these perspectives would include valuing behaviors such as empathy, sensitivity, self-discipline, tolerance, and building positive social relationships with individuals of all ages.

What does it mean to care? Caring is a thoughtful, empathetic concern for the world around us. It is an all-inclusive term that is reflective of a custodial attitude for the protection of humans as well as a regard for the environment. Children who care are open to others by respecting their rights and ideas, accepting differences, and being trustworthy and generous. Understanding and valuing others in addition to self is an important step in the caring process.

Building caring attitudes through social and emotional learning is an essential component of any social studies curriculum in primary and intermediate grades. Children develop the knowledge, skills, and values that build a caring community through civic action at increasingly complex levels throughout their schooling. This caring community is inclusive of the self, home, school, neighborhood, nation, and world. Implementation of designed classroom activities has great potential for nurturing this caring community.

Although developing a caring community should be a concern throughout the elementary curriculum, it is a basic embodiment of the social studies curriculum. Fostering caring attitudes and behaviors as essential components of the social studies curriculum in the primary and intermediate grades plays a central role in the essence of elementary programs. To guide educators through the implementation of a caring curriculum, a graphic organizer is provided.

To symbolize the *Learning to Care Paradigm*, circles within a triangle are chosen. The caring community of learners in the center of the inner circle, *Students*, becomes the focus of the curriculum. The outer circle represents *The Universal Declaration of Human Rights* (United Nations Department of Public Information, 1998), as adopted and proclaimed by the General Assembly of the United Nations in 1948, that together with the National Council for the Social Studies (NCSS) Standards serve as the conceptual framework to structure the caring dimensions of this book. Some developmental concepts derived from the Articles found in the *Declaration* include freedom, equality, justice, democracy, peace, individual and group rights, due process under the law, global citizenship, personal and social responsibility, and respect for others. The NCSS Ten Thematic Strands in Social Studies that include Culture (I), Time, Continuity, and Change (II), People, Places, and Environments (III), Individual Development and Identity (IV), Individuals, Groups, and Institutions (V), Power, Authority, and Governance (VI), Production, Distribution, and Consumption (VII), Science, Technology, and Society (VIII), Global Connections (IX), and Civic Ideals and Practices (X) are used as interrelated themes drawn from the social science and other related disciplines and provide a framework for social studies instruction. These documents serve to guide and support the three other components (*Teachers*, *Literature*, and *Activities*) affecting curriculum implementation.

Learning to Care Paradigm

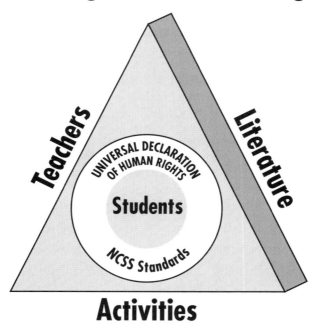

The *Teacher* uses the document as a guide to choose the appropriate *Literature* that would represent one or more of the concepts that are important for children to know and act on. Next, using the selected trade book as a basis, the teacher designs relevant *Activities* that focus on developing the anticipated student knowledge, skills, and values.

All adults in the school environment must be encouraged to embody and model for students these conceptual values through awareness, communication, and education. This book, however, is geared for K–6 teachers because of their unique function in the cognitive and affective learning process of youngsters. Through the implementation of suggested strategies within the disciplines of the social studies curriculum (history, anthropology, geography, sociology, political science, economics, law, and psychology), teachers can assist children in building a personal and collective identity. The integration of literature throughout the activities serves as the connection to caring and civic action in children.

Books have always played a role in a student's life both at home and at school to inform and entertain. It is the authors' contention that the use of various genre of children's literature facilitates the understanding of caring within the milieu of community.

To foster caring attitudes among children, fiction and nonfiction literature have been selected and related expository and expressive activities provided. Books of prose and verse were included among the fiction genre selected while concept and information books as well as biographies constituted the nonfiction trade books. In both types, we have included a variety of books, traditional favorites and current notable books, that are appropriate for the selected age and interests of the children. Not only are these books quality examples of children's literature, but they are also apropos to the caring theme. They included major characters with whom the children could easily identify because they shared similar qualities to the young reader. This identification is a necessary component for the development of empathy. As major characters in many picture storybooks for primary-grade readers tend to be animals or inanimate objects, the stories chosen for this book clearly expressed and illustrated human feelings, hopes, and action that could facilitate identification, for example *My Town* and *The Little House*.

The selected literature was adapted to support expressive and expository activities that align with moral concepts from the Articles of the *Universal Declaration of Human Rights*. It is from this human perspective that a book may be concerned with a part of a universal right and not all of its identified components. To facilitate the students' understanding of an Article, the abbreviated *Student Resource Sheet: Universal Declaration of Human Rights* established by the University of Minnesota Peace Resource Center (n.d.), was used as the structure recommended in the Caring Connections and Caring Corner. In addition, the NCSS Ten Thematic Strands in Social Studies serve as a framework for the activities provided throughout the book. The activities enable children to become involved in action projects that make a difference. The final outcome is social action that supports the caring values and behavior so desperately needed in their world.

As children have individual experiences, they view the world from personal and collective perspectives. The chapter titles reflect these perspectives by using "My" to precede the dimensions of self and family, while "Our" is used to represent the collective sense as part of the larger environment such as school, neighborhood, nation, and world. To illustrate the caring dimensions within these perspectives, some types of literature were better suited to the titles and themes of chapters than others. For the personal perspective, in the chapter titled "My Self" such books as *Judy Moody* and *Different Just Like Me* were selected because they portray children overcoming personal problems and working toward feelings of self-confidence and worth. To support the collective perspective, historical fiction, for example, was frequently used in "Our Nation" so that the readers could grasp the notion of our nation's past accomplishments and failures in caring for its citizens. In *Baseball Saved Us*, how the Nation made a grave error was represented when loyal Japanese-American citizens were sent to internment camps. The lives of slave families in the antebellum South were movingly expressed in *Nettie's Journey South*. Stories concerning the symbols, celebrations, and heroes throughout our history were included in such books as *My Dream of Martin Luther King* and *The Flag We Love*. The books used for "Our World" centered on caring and global connections with special attention to similarities between children of different cultures, the inhumanity that occurs during national conflicts and wars, and the importance of safeguarding the world's natural resources. *Common Ground: The Water, Earth, and Air We Share* was used as a book for primary-aged students that focused on sharing resources among all people.

Each chapter is formatted into four sections: Caring Circle, Caring Connection, Caring Corner, and Caring Collection. The Caring Circle introduces each chapter and provides the common parameters that establish the foundations for the concept of caring in each dimension, the role of caring, and action behavior related to the specific environments. These foundations are supported by the research in education and other disciplines as well as the authors' own observations and experiences with children.

Caring Connections provides the reader with authors, titles, and genre of books for appropriate grade levels: K–6. For each book selected the Title, Author, Genre, Level, Reader, and The Book (brief synopsis) are given. Forming the framework for activities are the relevant Human Rights Article(s) and related NCSS Standard(s). Factors identified for each book include Knowledge, Skills, and Values. Knowledge encompasses the expected cognitive outcomes. Anticipated cognitive, affective, and psychomotor abilities are noted under Skills. The Values section refers to the likely outcomes in affective and social dispositions.

Activities were developed for three levels: Primary (K–2), Bridge (2–4), and Intermediate (4–6). The "bridge" level was intentionally included to span the gap between primary and intermediate readers to better meet the needs of lower and higher achievers. Each activity section is structured for higher-order thinking skills as well as three modes of participation: I = Individual (student working independently), P = Partner (two or more students working together), G = Group (class participating as a whole).

Expressive and expository activities integrate the arts, English language arts, social studies, science, math, and technology. When integrating the arts with English language arts, a few expressive activities might be that the students could mime the characters, write and act out skits, and construct puppets to creatively express ideas found in the books. The use of technology in the form of computers, videotape, and digital cameras enhances factual oral and written projects for expository activities.

The I-BE-IT Model frames expressive and expository activities appropriate to fiction and nonfiction trade books specifically designed for developing caring attitudes and behaviors. The model's structure evolved from a phenomenological approach that uses an analytical method for analyzing and articulating the feelings experienced during personal situations and developmental bibliotherapy that emphasizes empathy. Examples of the I-BE-IT are found in activities for *The Story of Ruby Bridges* in the chapter, "Our School," and *On the Wings of Eagles* in "Our World." We recommend that I-BE-IT be used with children in the intermediate grades.

The activities for each book were products of the authors' education, research, and classroom experiences. Many were implemented and assessed by professors, classroom teachers, and education majors at professional development school sites. Photographs of children who participated in some of the activities at various school sites were included in the chapters. In addition, appropriate sample reproducible art following the related activities is provided at the end of each chapter.

The Caring Corner section provides the reader with synopses of additional trade books appropriate for the caring environments addressed in the aforementioned chapters. The teacher is provided with the related Human Rights Articles and NCSS Standards for each book. In this section, teachers can make use of these additional books in creating their own related activities.

The Caring Collection lists full citations for all Caring Connections and Caring Corner selections used at the conclusion of each chapter. These and other sources for educators to use in creating a caring community are included by relevant chapter headings in the references.

CHAPTER 1

My Self

CARING CIRCLE

My Self

The self is the honey of all beings,
and all beings are the honey of the self.
—Brehadaranyaka Upanishad, 1.3.28

The Concept of Self

Although children share similar characteristics in their growth and development, each child is unique as an individual. A child's conception of self is the interaction and interdependence of the cognitive, emotional, social, and physical self. How a child reacts to these features of self results in a variety of attitudes, behaviors, and values. It is important for a child to develop early in life a positive attitude toward self through a genuine awareness and understanding of these features in addition to having supportive experiences within the personal environment. A child with a positive self-concept comes not only to care for the personal self but also to care for others during childhood and beyond.

The Role of Caring for Self

Self-acceptance and self-confidence comes from having a positive self-concept. Thus, a child develops feelings of being worthwhile, trustworthy, responsible, and liked by others. A growth of confidence in self results in the ability to construct new knowledge, work collaboratively, accept others, and be accepted in social situations. An inability to care for self may lead to social isolation and antisocial behaviors, such as a lack of sensitivity and empathy as well as hostility toward others. It is evident, therefore, that caring for self plays a relevant role in bringing about caring for others.

Taking Personal Action

Individual responsibility for caring requires that the child undergo an ongoing process of self-awareness, self-management, and self-assessment of attitudes and values. Guided by these actions, a child makes a personal commitment to caring behaviors that include being sensitive to the needs of others, respecting individual rights, working cooperatively, and being a contributor to the well-being of family, school, neighborhood, and national and world community.

CARING CONNECTION

Bad Hair Day

The Connection: *Bad Hair Day* by Susan Hood, 1999
Genre: Picture Storybook
Level: Primary
Reader: Teacher & Student
The Book: Geared for the beginning reader, this simply worded story told of a young girl who was upset by her mother's inept cutting of her hair. Afraid that others would make fun of her, she hid this mistake under a wide-brimmed, red hat. On her trip to the hairdresser to fix her "bad" hair, she saw a variety of people with different hairdos and came to the understanding that everyone was unique. People didn't have to have the same type of hairstyle. The next day, at school, her newly styled hair was admired by her classmates. The youngster realized that having a bad hair day was not a complete disaster. It could lead to good things happening.

Human Rights Article(s):

Article 2: Freedom from discrimination

NCSS Standard(s):

IV. Individual Development and Identity

Knowledge:
- Describe the feelings that the girl in the story had about the haircut her mother gave her.
- Describe personal feelings about having a bad hair day.
- Explain the sight of various hairdos and the impression made on the girl.
- Detail how the girl felt about going to school with her new haircut.
- Relate personal experiences about being admired, laughed at, or teased by classmates concerning appearance.

Skills:
- Gather information about the various hairstyles among males and females of all ages.
- Classify the hairstyles according to length, style, and color.
- Match individual hairstyles in chart form.
- Evaluate personal hairstyle preferences and the relationship to feelings about self.

Value(s): Individual feelings of self-worth are supported by behaviors not appearances.

Activities: I = Individual   P = Partners   G = Group

A. Hat Full of Feelings (I, G)

Materials: large hat for bulletin board, small hat pattern, construction paper, pencils, scissors, crayons, yarn, stapler

After reading the book, the teacher discusses the feelings the girl has about her appearance. Students discuss feelings they have experienced about their own appearance. They will be creating "hat" pictures that represent a time when they had particular feelings, good or bad, about their own appearance. Using a regular paper size hat pattern, have children trace the pattern on construction paper and cut out the hat. With crayons, they will draw a picture of that "feeling time." In front of the bulletin board displaying a large colorful hat, the children will share their feeling pictures and then with yarn, hang the picture hat from the brim of the large bulletin board hat. Conduct a discussion using the following questions.

Questions to Ask:
1. How did the girl in the story feel about her new haircut? Why?
2. How would you feel about a new haircut? Explain.
3. Why did the girl feel somewhat better after seeing different hairstyles and colors?
4. Why did the girl feel nervous about going to school with her new haircut?
5. How could you help the girl feel better about herself if she was in your school?

A Hat Full of Feelings

B. Hair-Raising Chart (P, G)

Materials: magazines with lots of hair, scissors, white glue, 11 x 17 construction paper, pencils, digital or instant camera/film

In pairs, students search through magazines for pictures of people with a variety of hairstyles and colors and cut out those of interest. On the large tri-folded construction paper, glue the pictures under the appropriately labeled columns: length, color, style (i.e., braids, buzz cut, etc.). Using a digital or instant camera, the teacher photographs each individual. The photos are then glued to the bottom of the chart matching length, color, and style by drawing a line between the photo and a similar magazine cut out. Partners show and share the charts explaining how they are similar to and uniquely different from the magazine pictures.

C. Hair-Raising Stories (I)

Materials: pencils, lined story paper cut in hat-shape, colored construction paper for covers, yarn, white glue, crayons, pencils, one-hole punch, metal clip rings

Children should be directed to write a story about a boy or girl coming to class with a new hairstyle different from everyone else. The story should close with ways that the individual will show acceptance to the child with the unique hairstyle and describe the resultant feelings experienced. Using the hat-shaped story lined paper, children write or dictate their information and draw a picture for each page. Be aware of the writing process and possible editing time before adding covers to the stories. Punch the side and insert the rings. Display the published books and allow the students to view and read each one independently.

The Big Box

The Connection: *The Big Box* by Toni Morrison & Slade Morrison, 1999
Genre: Picture Storybook
Level: Bridge
Reader: Teacher & Student
The Book: This powerful story about three children, Patty, Mickey, and Liza Sue, yearning for individual freedom, was written from a child's perspective. As they acted on their impulses, adults sought to limit their freedoms by placing them in *the big box*. The children felt confined and lacked the ability to determine their own destiny. Although the box contained all things that children love, they were forbidden to do the one thing they wanted to do most, to go outside the box and actually experience running free.

Human Rights Article(s):

Article 3: Right to life, liberty, personal security

Article 5: Freedom from torture, degrading treatment

Article 13: Right to free movement in and out of the country

Article 19: Freedom of opinion and information

NCSS Standard(s):

IV. Individual Development and Identity

V. Individuals, Groups, and Institutions

Knowledge:

- Describe the behaviors and the resultant limitations set on personal freedoms for the children in the book.
- Describe the feelings of the children during their confinement in "the box."
- Detail your own behaviors and the resultant limitations set on your personal freedom.
- Describe your feelings about losing personal freedom.
- Compare the behaviors and feelings of the children in the book when they lost personal freedom to your own experiences.

Skills:

- Gather data about personal freedom, consequences of actions, and resultant feelings from the book characters, yourself, and classmates.
- Classify the data into positive and negative consequences.
- Interpret which personal freedoms are acceptable and which ones may infringe on the personal freedoms of others.
- Evaluate those appropriate personal behaviors in terms of positive impact on self.
- Formulate principles that may expand personal freedom for selves and others.

Value(s): Personal freedom within appropriate limitations promotes self-respect, self-esteem, and caring for others.

Activities: I = Individual   P = Partners   G = Group

A. Behavior Box (I, G)

Materials: chart paper, markers

After reading the book, children discuss the actions and consequences of Mickey, Patty, and Liza Sue. Using a think-pair-share strategy for discussion, have students consider their own actions (student makes a comment that made everyone laugh) and the resultant consequences (teacher praised the student's humor or sent student to time out for disrupting the class) as well as make comparisons to the children in the book. Divide the chart paper into three columns labeling them Plus, Minus, and Maybe (PMM). In the Plus column, record those actions that resulted in positive consequences. In the Minus column, record those actions that resulted in negative consequences. For Maybe, record actions that may or may not fit the Plus or Minus columns depending on the situation. Using the PMM Chart discuss the following questions.

Questions to Ask:
1. What did Patty, Mickey, and Liza Sue do to be put in the big box?
2. How did they feel about losing their freedom?
3. In what behaviors did you engage that resulted in a plus or a minus on the chart?
4. How did you feel about losing your freedom?
5. Why did you lose your personal freedom when you behaved in a way that others did not appreciate?
6. How could the children in the book avoid losing their personal freedom?
7. How could you avoid losing personal freedom?
B. In the Box (I)

Materials: shoebox with cover, index paper (70 weight), miniatures, crayons or markers, paper, pencils

Ask the students to reflect on a behavior in which they engaged that resulted in time out or privileges being taken away. Have them use pencil and paper to draw a rendering of the site and objects (furniture, toys, window, door, etc.) within this site. Using a shoebox, children construct a bird's-eye view of this site in diorama format. Cover the lid with construction paper and label with appropriate title. Each child has the opportunity to display and describe the diorama to classmates.

B. Avoiding the Box (I, P)

Materials: personal journal, chart paper, markers

After reviewing and reflecting on the PMM Chart and dioramas, partner groups of at least three members brainstorm a list of ideas that have the potential for avoiding the box. Evaluate which ideas do not infringe on the freedom of others and will likely result in positive consequences for themselves and others. Each partner group creates a list of ideas and presents it to the class. Based on the partner-group lists, individuals select ideas to carry out and reflect on the results in personal journals. They should identify the action, result, and feelings concerning implementation of "avoiding the box" actions. The journals should be ongoing so the students can make substantive changes in behavior.

Judy Moody

The Connection: *Judy Moody* by Megan McDonald, 2000

Genre: Fiction, Chapter Book

Level: Bridge

Reader: Student

The Book: Judy Moody was anxious about going to third grade with a new teacher and all the changes that would accompany the experience. Her bad mood was heightened by a "know-it-all" brother who was entering her beloved second grade. Things got even worse when her new teacher assigned a Me collage. A number of disagreeable events occurred on the way to completing this assignment that do not improve her mood. When the Jungle Juice was accidentally spilled onto her project, Judy's mood hit rock bottom. Despite the feeling that her collage was ruined, through her imagination she modified the presentation so her Me collage was well received. Because of her experiences, Judy gained a caring perspective for herself and others.

Human Rights Article(s)

Article 17: Right to own property

Article 19: Freedom of opinion and information

NCSS Standard(s):

IV. Individual Development and Identity

X. Civic Ideals and Practices

Knowledge:

- Describe the situations that brought about Judy's bad mood.
- Identify situations that contribute to personal bad moods.
- Explain how characters in the book helped Judy change her bad mood to good.
- Explain how Judy accepted the challenge of personal responsibility for her actions.

Skills:

- Classify Judy's moods into positive and negative categories.
- Analyze the catalysts for each related mood that Judy displayed.

- Summarize ways in which Judy took responsibility for her own negative mood and changed it into a positive experience.
- Present information in cause–and-effect "blue mood" stories generating ideas so that the characters change blue moods to positive experiences.
- In groups, share the impact of personal responsibility in controlling moods.

Value(s): Everyone shares in personal responsibility for feelings and moods for themselves as well as others.

Activities: I = Individual   P = Partners   G = Group

A. Mood Matters (G)

Materials: T-chart, markers

On chart paper, draw a t-chart labeling the first column + and the second column −. Title the chart "Moods." After reading the book, ask children to identify the situations that led to Judy's moods. Record the information on the t-chart making sure that good mood situations are listed under + and bad mood situations under −.

Questions to Ask:
1. How are Judy's moods similar to your own moods?
2. What situations have led to your personal moods?
3. In the book, how did Judy make a bad situation good?
4. How did the characters in the book help Judy change her mood?
5. Who contributed to changing your mood?
6. What did you personally do to support positive moods for yourself and for others?

B. Me Mood Collage (I)

Materials: markers, crayons, poster board, magazines, scissors, tape, white glue, other materials related to individual preference

Students gather ideas and materials showing the situations that directly relate to their personal good and bad moods. On the poster board, organize materials into sections for each type of mood labeling each area with a situation title. Use "Mood Situations" with the student name as the poster title. Students share the *Me Mood Collages* with the class relating the catalysts for their moods.

C. Blue Mood Stories (P, I)

Materials: construction paper, stapler, computer and printer, word processing and drawing software, scanner (optional)

Using the *Me Mood Collage* and *Mood Matters* chart as guides, discuss various situations in which good and bad moods were precipitated. Determine in partner groups the personal actions that could be taken to change bad moods to good moods. After this discussion, individual students reflect and write about situations that relate to personal bad moods. Then, to close the story, individuals write about the personal responsibility that could be taken to change blue moods to positive experiences. Each episode bears the situation title noted on the collage. In partner groups, share the personal responsibility that is required to change moods and to support others in changing moods, as well. Both the collage and book are displayed together so that others may read and learn from these experiences.

Different Just Like Me

The Connection: *Different Just Like Me* by Lori Mitchell, 1999

Genre: Picture Storybook

Level: Primary

Reader: Student

The Book: April, a young girl with a pigment disorder, had to wait a week before she visited her grandmother. She spent this week being an acute observer of people and objects. She noted the varieties of foods, flowers, animals, and abodes as well as the dissimilarities among humans such as size, appearance, race, and disabilities. Reflecting on all she had seen, April came to this happy conclusion——being different was okay.

Human Rights Article(s):

    Article 1: Right to equality

    Article 2: Freedom from discrimination

NCSS Standard(s):

    I. Culture

    IV. Individual Development and Identity

Knowledge:

- Identify how people from the book are similar to each other and to April.
- Describe ways in which children in your class are similar to each other.
- Describe the unique differences among people.
- Explain how unique differences make April and us special.

Skills:

- Gather information about the similarities among people in April's world and your own.
- Classify similarities among classmates according to food, games, television shows, and toys.
- Analyze how the unique differences among people in April's world make them special.
- Discover and evaluate a unique personal difference that makes each student special.

Value(s): Being different makes everyone special.

Activities: I = Individual   P = Partners   G = Group

A. Window on My World (I, G)

Materials: "Window on My World" reproducible, pencils, crayons, scissors, tape

After reading the book, each student chooses a favorite food, game/toy, television show, and activity and draws it in the corresponding box on the reproducible. Cut out each box and bring these to the full-group setting. Students share their favorites with each other while posting them in the four categories with like favorites in the same columns forming a picture graph of similarities.

Questions to Ask:

1. How are your favorites like your classmates?
2. Which favorites are special to only a few students?
3. How are your favorites like April's? How are they different?
4. What is there about April makes her special and "great?"
5. What is there about you that makes you special and "great?"

B. Sign Me Special (P, G)

Materials: sign language alphabet, the book

Discuss with students the pages in the book illustrating the use of sign language among persons with hearing impairments. The importance of using sign language to communicate should be emphasized. Using the letters and signs on the sign language alphabet, students choose the signs that correspond to their own initials. Teacher and other helpers work with children, in partners, to facilitate the finger formations required for each initial. Partners practice with each other until proficient then share with the entire group. Have students talk about how knowing sign language is great.

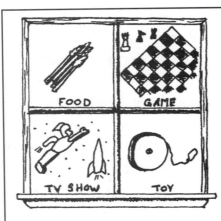

Figure 1.1
Window
on My World

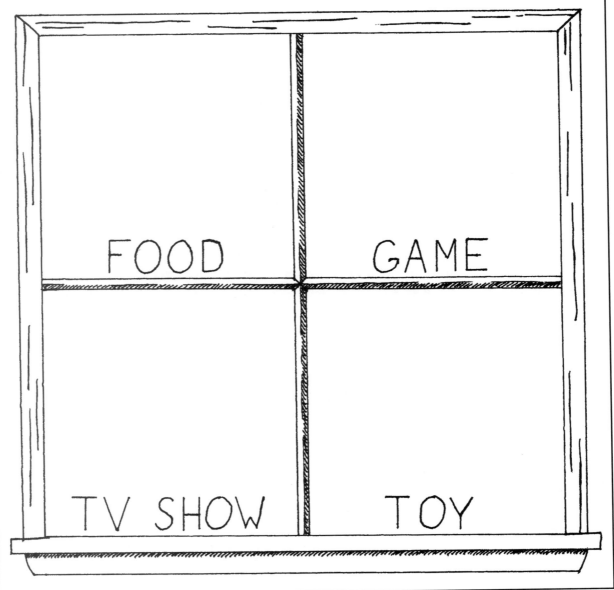

FOOD

GAME

TV SHOW

TOY

C. ME-dallions (I)

Materials: copy of Braille alphabet, ribbon, round cookie cutter, pencils, small beads for decorations, scissors, waxed paper, flour-salt-water dough, markers, reproducible

Using the Braille illustration from the book as a guide, discuss with the children the use of alternative written communication used by persons with visual impairments. Show the children a copy of the Braille alphabet and have them feel the letters for their first initials. Tell the students that they will be making ME-dallions (see "ME-dallions" reproducible for instructions) with their first initials in Braille using a dough mixture. When completed, students may wear their ME-dallions and share with others their understanding of the important role of alternative communication for persons with visual impairment.

A Boy Called Slow

The Connection: *A Boy Called Slow* by Joseph Bruchac, 1998
Genre: Picture Storybook
Level: Intermediate
Reader: Student
The Book: Among the Lakota Sioux, it was traditional to name children by their actions. The only son of the warrior, Returns Again, was given the name Slow, because his every action was slow. Throughout his childhood, Slow was unhappy with his name and was eager to prove himself by being brave and wise so he could gain a new, more honorable name. He was given the opportunity at the age of fourteen when he was allowed to join a war party against an old enemy, the Crow. Slow surprised his fellow warriors by jumping into action to lead the charge against the Crow. Because of the success of this raid, Slow was bestowed with his new name Tatan'ka Iyota'ke, Sitting Bull.

Human Rights Article(s):
    Article 6: Right to recognition as a person before the law
    Article 22: Right to social security
    Article 29: Community duties essential to free and full development

NCSS Standard(s):
    I. Culture
    II. Time, Continuity, and Change
    IV. Individual Development and Identity

Knowledge:
    • Identify the process of naming children in the Lakota culture.

Figure 1.2
ME-dallions

Creating ME-dallions takes a few simple materials and
a little creativity and patience.

Materials:

Copy of the Braille alphabet
Round cookie cutter
Waxed paper
Scissors
Flour-salt-water dough*
Rolling pin

Length of ¼-inch ribbon
Small glass craft beads
Spoon & bowl
Pencil
Tempera paint
White glue

*2 parts flour to 1 part salt and 1 part water

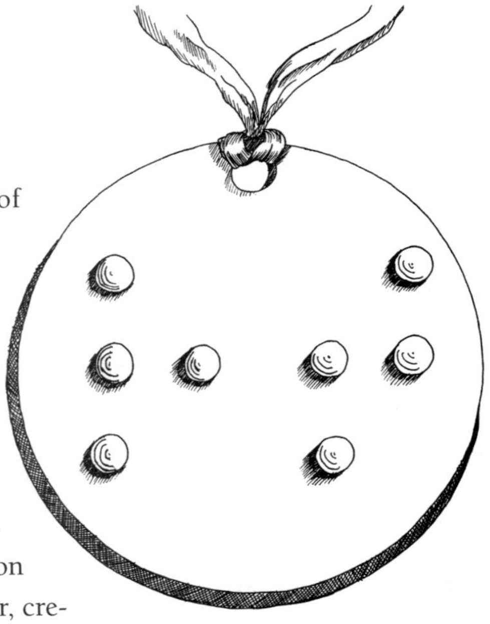

Directions:

Making Medallions

Mix flour and salt together in the bowl. Add enough of
the water to moisten the salt and flour mixture. Gradu-
ally add the remaining water (be sparing with the
water avoiding overly sticky clay) while mixing.
After the dough is thoroughly mixed, knead the clay
for 10 to 12 minutes until it is smooth. Break off
enough clay to form a medallion approximately 2–2½
inches in diameter. Knead a drop of tempera paint of a
personally chosen color into the dough. Once colored
dough is completed, wash and dry hands. Place dough on
the waxed paper and roll flat. Using a round cookie cutter, create the shape of the medallion.

Making ME-dallions

Consult the Braille alphabet for your first initial. After making a pencil impression, use the art
beads to form the design on the still damp clay. You may wish to use white glue for better
adherence before pressing the beads into the clay. Again, using the pencil, poke a hole near (not
too close) to the top of the medallion. Let it dry in a warm, dry location overnight or bake in a
warm oven (about 250°) for about an hour. Once dry, insert a length of ribbon through the hole.
Tie, and wear your ME-dallion.

- Describe how Slow felt about his given name.
- Explain the meaning behind personal given names.
- Describe how you feel about the meaning of your given name and its relationship to your true nature.
- Relate the way in which Slow changes his name to be more acceptable to his true self.
- Detail how this name change contributed to the well-being of his people.

Skills:

- Gather data about the origin of Lakota names and personal names.
- Compare and contrast the meanings behind personal and Lakota names.
- Analyze the cultural patterns concerning the time and manner in which the children are named.
- Analyze your given name as it relates to personal actions.
- Create and present an appropriate name related to personal accomplishments and contributions to others.
- Evaluate Slow's new name as it relates to his accomplishments and contributions to the Lakota people.

Value(s): Personal feelings about self are reflected in personal caring actions toward others.

Activities: I = Individual   P = Partners   G = Group

A. Meaning of Names (I, G)

Materials: the book, web-based computer, printer, comparison chart, markers

Individually, using the book, each student researches the origin and procedures used in naming Lakota children. On the computer, children find the traditional meanings to their personal names. Divide the chart paper into two columns, labeling one column, Lakota and the other column, Personal. Next, divide the paper into three Feature rows, labeling the first row as Time (when children are named——at birth), the second as Manner (how names are determined—— stylish), and the third as Meaning (what names represent——Michael = angelic). In a group discussion, students provide information to complete the comparison chart. Using the chart as a reference, respond to the following questions.

Questions to Ask:
1. In the time of the book, how and when did the Lakota name their children?
2. Today, how and when are most children named?
3. How did names represent actions for the Lakota?
4. How do names represent actions for you, today?

5. What are the similarities and differences evident between both cultures?
6. What feelings do you have for the meaning of your given name?
7. What feelings did Slow have about his given name and what action did he take?

B. New Names—New Frames (I)

Materials: matte board, white construction paper, acrylic markers, calligraphy pens, masking tape

Students, individually, reflect on past positive caring actions that could contribute to a new name (i.e., Michael loves to play basketball with his friends. As a team player, he makes a habit of passing the ball to a teammate who is position for a good shot rather than selfishly shooting). Once students have determined a behavior that is representative of themselves, they then create a new name in the Lakota tradition. Using the acrylic markers and construction paper, students draw a picture of themselves in action. Pictures should be matted for presentation. On the frame matte, students write their new meaningful name with the calligraphy pens. Students share with the class their new name accompanied by the rationale.

C. Personal Quest—Personal Best (I)

Materials: computer with word-processing program, printer, two pocket folders, table/desk

Students individually determine future actions that contribute to a more caring personal image as well as the well-being of others and relate directly to their chosen name. Once each one has identified three to five actions, type them in a large font on the computer and print out the sheet. The teacher should label each sheet with a letter of the alphabet (A–Z, depending on the number of children in the class) and place them in a folder. Hang the pictures from *New Names—New Frames* on a bulletin board and number each one sequentially. The teacher then creates a matching sheet with numbers 1–? corresponding to the numbers on the posted pictures making enough copies for each child. During free time, individual students read caring action sheets, review the New Names pictures for content, match caring actions to appropriate action pictures with names, and indicate matches on the matching sheet. The object of this activity is to help students understand the actions to take that would fulfill their commitment to the well-being of others. A full-group discussion should evaluate how the name chosen and the caring actions represent this commitment.

The Shakespeare Stealer

The Connection: *The Shakespeare Stealer* by Gary Blackwood, 1998

Genre: Historical Fiction, Chapter Book

Level: Intermediate

Reader: Student

The Book: Having survived the orphanage and his first prenticeship (a strict tutelage in cryptic shorthand), Widge found himself bought by a Mr. Bass. Knowing Widge's skill, Bass forced the youngster to go to London under the guard of the evil Falconer and copy Shakespeare's *Hamlet*. Bass's theatrical group would then perform the stolen work. Due to a variety of miscues, Widge found himself in the Globe Theatre Company as a prentice learning the intricacies of acting, swordplay, and costuming. Eventually, he had a starring-role performance in front of the Queen at court. Falconer hounded the youngster to steal the playbook. Widge was faced with a dilemma. His decision brought him, at long last, into a family and a real home.

Human Rights Article(s):

Article 3: Right to life, liberty, personal security

Article 4: Freedom from slavery

Article 23: Right to desirable work and to join trade unions

NCSS Standard(s):

I. Culture

II. Time, Continuity, and Change

IV. Individual Development and Identity

Knowledge:

- Describe the setting and culture of the theatre of Shakespeare during Widge's time.
- Explain the prentice system and its impact on Widge.
- Depict the role of Bass/Falconer and the nefarious plans as portrayed in the book.
- Identify the dilemma that Widge faces.

Skills:

- Gather information, from a variety of sources, about Widge's world of the Globe Theatre and the prentice system during the renaissance in England.
- Compare the knowledge and skills learned in the prentice system to that learned in schools today.
- Compare Widge's personal ethics to Bass's and classify according to standards of goodness and rightness.
- Evaluate Widge's solution to his dilemma.
- After developing common standards of goodness and rightness, construct a play based on a dilemma and has a resolution that meets those standards.

Value(s): Ethical and moral decisions are made according to standards of goodness and rightness.

Activities: I = Individual   P = Partners   G = Group

A. Standards of Rightness and Goodness (G)

Materials: chart paper, markers

Using the book, discuss Widge's standards of rightness and goodness and compare them to those of Bass/Falconer as well as the children in the class. Determine the relationship of the *Universal Declaration of Human Rights* to rightness and goodness. On a chart divided into three columns labeled *Widge*, *Bass/Falconer*, and *Our Class*, list standards that fit each one. Drawing information from the chart, personal experiences, and the book, answer the following questions.

Questions to Ask:
1. According to the chart, who maintains standards of rightness and goodness? Explain your response.
2. What dilemma did Widge face that called on him to use his personal standards of rightness and goodness?
3. What was Widge's solution to his dilemma? What would you do?
4. Why did Widge decide to solve his dilemma as he did?
5. What do you think of his solution? Explain.

B. Virtues' Journal (G, I)

Materials: small marble notebook, pen, chart paper, markers, computer, printer http://www.amnesty-usa.org/aikids

As a class, determine generic standards of rightness and goodness using personal experiences, the book, the data collected, and the *Universal Declaration of Human Rights (AiKids Plain Language Version)*. List common standards as agreed to by the class on the chart paper for reference purposes. Print a copy for students to staple to a page in their journals. Throughout the year, students are to write of experiences in which they face and resolve dilemmas based on the standards of rightness and goodness. Meeting in groups, weekly discussions of their journal entries should take place. At the end of the year, students reflect on their journal entries and determine the effectiveness of their standards in coming to resolution.

C. Participation Playlet (P)

Materials: virtues journal, legal pads, pencils, pens, playlet reproducible

Working in cooperative partner groups and using the virtues journal, students identify a moral dilemma as a focus for a dramatic presentation set in modern time and written in playlet form. The playlet is a one-act, five- to eight-minute play that may have two to five scenes and a minimum of three characters. The minor characters representing goodness and badness set the scene for the dilemma. The information is recorded on the playlet reproducible. The major character is faced with making a moral decision about the dilemma based on the standards of rightness and goodness. The audience has the responsibility of helping the character resolve the dilemma. The presenting partner group determines the appropriate time to stop the play (all minor characters freeze) so that the major character can discuss the situation with the audience. Once consensus about resolution has been reached, the play continues to its conclusion. After the playlet has ended, all students should evaluate the drama and decision made based on the standards of rightness and goodness found in their virtues journal to determine if the best resolution to the dilemma was made.

Participation Playlet

CARING CORNER

Cinder-Elly

The Connection: *Cinder-Elly* by Frances Minters, 1997

Genre: Picture Storybook

Level: Primary

Reader: Teacher & Student

The Book: In this updated, verse version of the famous tale, Cinder-Elly lived in New York City with her parents and mean sisters who kept her from accompanying them to the game to see the star, Prince Charming, play basketball. Fairy Godmother appeared waving the magic wand that turned Cinder-Elly into a cool chick with a red miniskirt, bracelets, and glass sneakers. A chance meeting with the prince brought about an offer for a pizza date that unfortunately never came about. Cinder-Elly's time ran out, and the prince was left holding the glass sneaker. Through modern technology, the prince made contact with the girl whose foot fit perfectly into the glass sneaker. Before the couple departed on their date, Cinder-Elly forgave her mean sisters.

Human Rights Article(s):

Article 2: Freedom from discrimination

Article 12: Freedom from interference with privacy, family, home, and correspondence

NCSS Standard(s):

I. Culture

IV. Individual Development and Identity

Feelings

The Connection: *Feelings* by Aliki, 1984

Genre: Picture Storybook

Level: Primary

Reader: Teacher

The Book: Aliki has created a delightful, yet insightful, book appropriate for primary-grade students. The illustrations depict typical situations that happen to children and the resultant positive or negative feelings with which they could readily identify and empathize. Particularly effective was the centerfold picture of the youngster and his teddy bear lying in the grass having a quiet moment between the pages experiencing feelings of joy and sadness.

Human Rights Article(s):

Article 1: Right to equality

Article 29: Community duties essential to free and full development

NCSS Standard(s):

    I. Culture

  IV. Individual Development and Identity

The Biggest Klutz in the Fifth Grade

The Connection: *The Biggest Klutz in the Fifth Grade* by Bill Wallace, 1994

        Genre: Fiction, Chapter Book

         Level: Intermediate

      Reader: Student

     The Book: Being flabby, overweight, and uncoordinated, not only made things happen to Pat (falls, bruises, broken bones) but also caused him to be called a klutz. A collision with a chain-link fence resulted in a challenge by Neal, the athlete, that Pat could not survive a summer of vigorous activities without hurting himself. If he failed, he had to complete an embarrassing feat in front of the entire school on the first day of classes. Determined to win and backed by his friends, Pat survived all of Neal's challenges. Discouraged, Neal set up one more dangerous activity that goaded Pat into retaliating against him and led to yet another injury. Although apparently a loser, Pat discovered that there can be rewards in losing.

Human Rights Article(s):

      Article 1: Right to equality

      Article 3: Right to life, liberty, personal security

      Article 5: Freedom from torture, degrading treatment

NCSS Standard(s):

  IV. Individual Development and Identity

Marguerite Makes a Book

The Connection: *Marguerite Makes a Book* by Bruce Robertson, 1999

        Genre: Historical Fiction, Picture Storybook

         Level: Intermediate

      Reader: Student

     The Book: Marguerite was the daughter of an Early Renaissance, Parisian, manuscript illuminator. An accident to her father's glasses necessitated that Marguerite complete a commissioned prayer book for Lady Isabelle. Although she was a female in a male-dominated craft, Marguerite showed courage and steadfastness as she began the painting process from purchasing proper parchment, mixing ink in paints, drawing and illustrating the margins, and painting a small portrait of the noble patron. Marguerite's success was due to not only caring for her craft, but also it was the caring for herself that gave her the confidence to complete the work.

Human Rights Article(s):

  Article 23: Right to desirable work and to join trade unions

  Article 27: Right to participate in the cultural life of the community

NCSS Standard(s):

 I. Culture

 II. Time, Continuity, and Change

 IV. Individual Development and Identity

Running Out of Time

The Connection: *Running Out of Time* by Margaret Peterson Haddix, 1997

  Genre: Fiction, Chapter Book

  Level: Intermediate

  Reader: Student

  The Book: It was 1840 in the village of Clifton and many children including Jessie's brother and sister were ill with diphtheria and there was no medicine. One evening, Jessie's mother told her a surprising secret that was known only to the adults. It was really 1996 and Clifton was a reconstructed historical site where tourists observed the residents who were isolated and prevented from returning to the present-time world. Jessie's mother sent her on a dangerous quest. She must escape the confines of the prisonlike fence, bring back medicine, and make their predicament known. Her adventure was harrowing for Jessie not only entered an unknown world of cars, phones, and blue jeans, but also evil genetic researchers who were trying to eliminate her. Jessie called upon her inner strength and courage to accomplish her quest and to save the children of Clifton.

Human Rights Article(s):

  Article 3: Right to life, liberty, personal security

  Article 5: Freedom from torture, degrading treatment

  Article 13: Right to free movement in and out of the country

  Article 19: Freedom of opinion and information

NCSS Standard(s):

 I. Culture

 II. Time, Continuity, and Change

 IV. Individual Development and Identity

 V. Individuals, Groups, and Institutions

Silent Lotus

The Connection: *Silent Lotus* by Jean M. Lee, 1991
Genre: Picture Storybook
Level: Primary, Bridge
Reader: Teacher & Student
The Book: Lotus, a young girl who was mute, lived in ancient Kampuchea. When other girls played, they ignored her and that made her lonely and unhappy. Her parents took her to the temple to pray for a solution. While there, Lotus felt the vibrations of the drums and imitated the motions of the dancers. The king and queen were so impressed that they provided a dance teacher and assured Lotus's parents that she would learn to dance. Imitating the herons, cranes, and white egrets, she became a renowned dancer and performed in temples and palaces throughout the land. Now, Lotus, not only had fame, but also friends.

Human Rights Article(s):
    Article 2: Freedom from discrimination
    Article 27: Right to participate in the cultural life of community

NCSS Standard(s):
    I. Culture
    IV. Individual Development and Identity

Randall's Wall

The Connection: *Randall's Wall* by Carol Fenner, 1991
Genre: Fiction, Chapter Book
Level: Intermediate
Reader: Student
The Book: Beset by an abusive, frequently absent father, a constantly sick mother, extreme poverty (no running water, little food, insufficient clothing), and the cruel taunts of his peers, Randall, a fifth grader built an invisible wall around himself that isolated him from the cold, uncaring world. Here he felt safe and worthwhile and was able to dream of better, beautiful things that were evidenced in his artistic talent. Saving the new girl from an attack by bullies, Randall gained a new friend who really cared about what happened to him. His security wall began to crack. It really collapsed when the discovery of his drawings resulted in a new lifestyle as well as a positive conception of himself.

Human Rights Article(s):
    Article 2: Freedom from discrimination
    Article 25: Right to an adequate living standard
    Article 27: Right to participate in the cultural life of community

NCSS Standard(s):

    I. Culture

   IV. Individual Development and Identity

    V. Individuals, Groups, and Institutions

The Midwife's Apprentice

The Connection: *The Midwife's Apprentice* by Karen Cushman, 1995

Genre: Historical Fiction, Chapter Book

Level: Intermediate

Reader: Student

The Book: The midwife, Jean Sharpe, in a medieval village, found a starving orphan girl keeping warm in a dung heap, brought her home to work, and dubbed her Beetle. Frightened that she would be turned out, the girl worked tirelessly from dawn to dusk, her only companion being a stray cat. Yearning to learn, the girl, who named herself Alyce, secretly observed the skills of the midwife and used this meager knowledge when she unexpectedly delivered her first baby. Considering herself stupid and a failure for having to call in the midwife for help on her first lone assignment, Alyce ran away to work as a tavern maid. There she had two encounters that changed her feelings about herself and her direction in life. She returned to Mistress Sharpe as a true apprentice to learn the art of midwifery.

Human Rights Article(s):

    Article 1: Right to equality

    Article 2: Freedom from discrimination

  Article 19: Freedom of opinion and information

  Article 23: Right to desirable work and to join trade unions

NCSS Standard(s):

    I. Culture

   II. Time, Continuity, and Change

   IV. Individual Development and Identity

Abbie Against the Storm

The Connection: *Abbie Against the Storm* by Marcia Vaughn, 1999

Genre: Picture Storybook

Level: Intermediate

Reader: Student

The Book: Based on a true story, a young girl, Abbie Burgess lived with her family on an island in Maine. As the lighthouse keeper, her father trained an enthusiastic Abbie in the skills of maintaining and lighting the globes. When he had to go to the mainland for much need food and supplies, Abbie was left in charge. She soon was faced with a crisis; a storm of great magnitude began to pummel the shore and darken the sky. Throughout the raging storm she had to keep the lanterns lit, the windows free of ice, the animals protected, and her family safe. Despite earlier qualms about her ability to keep the lights burning, she found the inner strength to successfully carry out all of her responsibilities.

Human Rights Article(s):
    Article 1: Right to equality
    Article 23: Right to desirable work and to join trade unions

NCSS Standard(s):
    II. Time Continuity and Change
    IV. Individual Development and Identity

I Like to Win!

The Connection: *I Like to Win!* by Charnan Simon, 1999
    Genre: Picture Storybook
    Level: Primary
    Reader: Student
    The Book: The smug, uncaring play behaviors of a young girl upset her brother who in turn got angry and refused to play further. Discovering that it was better to play with him than by herself, she changed her attitude, made an agreement with her playmate, and both continued to have fun playing games together.

Human Rights Article(s):
    Article 19: Freedom of opinion and information

NCSS Standard(s):
    IV. Individual Development and Identity

You Are Special

The Connection: *You Are Special* by Mac Lucado, 1997
    Genre: Picture Storybook
    Level: Primary, Bridge
    Reader: Teacher & Student
    The Book: The Wemmicks, the wooden people carved by Eli, were all of different intellects, sizes, appearances, and skills. The wooden ones spent their days sticking gold dots on

the beautiful and talented people to make them feel good and superior. Gray dots were placed on those who were not, so they felt worthless and miserable. Punchinello was one of the latter. To his surprise, he encountered Lucia who had no dots, for dots would not stick on her. He wanted to be just like Lucia. Punchinello visited Eli who told him that he didn't care what the Wemmicks thought. To Eli, his maker, he was very special. He told Punchinello to trust in his love and to care less about the stickers. This personal enlightenment led to the fulfillment of his personal wish.

Human Rights Article(s):
>   Article 2:   Freedom from discrimination
>   Article 5:   Freedom from torture and degrading treatment
>   Article 18:   Freedom of belief and religion

NCSS Standard(s):
> IV. Individual Development and Identity
>   V. Individuals, Groups, and Institutions

Mirette on the High Wire

The Connection: *Mirette on the High Wire* by Emily Arnold McCully, 1992
Genre: Picture Storybook
Level: Bridge
Reader: Student
The Book: In Paris in the late nineteenth century lived a young girl, Mirette, with her mother who ran a boarding house for actors and other performers. One day, when Mirette saw the new boarder, Bellini, walking a tight rope, she attempted to imitate his movements on the wire. Despite many failed attempts, she did succeed and was noticed by Bellini. He taught her some professional moves on the wire. Mirette discovered that he was once famous as a high-wire artist who had lost his nerve. To gain Mirette's admiration for his work, Bellini set up a new high-wire stunt between the roofs of two buildings. While on the wire, he froze from fear but was able to overcome it when the courageous Mirette joined him.

Human Rights Article(s):
>   Article 3:   Right to life, liberty, personal security
>   Article 23:   Right to desirable work and to join trade unions

NCSS Standard(s):
>   II. Time, Continuity, and Change
> IV. Individual Development and Identity

CARING COLLECTION: SELF

Aliki. (1984). *Feelings*. New York: HarperCollins Publishers.

Blackwood, G. (1998). *The Shakespeare Stealer*. New York: Puffin Books.

Bruchac, J. (1998). *A Boy Called Slow*. New York: Scott Foresman.

Cushman, K. (1995). *The Midwife's Apprentice*. New York: HarperCollins Publishers.

Fenner, C. (1991). *Randall's Wall*. New York: Aladdin Paperbacks.

Haddix, M. P. (1997). *Running Out of Time*. New York: Aladdin Paperbacks.

Hood, S. (1999). *Bad Hair Day*. New York: The Putnam & Grosset Group.

Lee, J. M. (1991). *Silent Lotus*. New York: Farrar, Straus & Giroux.

Lucado, M. (1997). *You Are Special*. Wheaton, IL: Crossway Books.

McCully, E. A. (1992). *Mirette on the High Wire*. New York: G. P. Putnam's Sons.

McDonald, M. (2000). *Judy Moody*. Cambridge, MA: Candlewick Press.

Minters, F. (1997). *Cinder-Elly*. New York: Puffin Books.

Mitchell, L. (1999). *Different Just Like Me*. Watertown, MA: Charlesbridge Publishing.

Morrison, T., & Morrison, S. (1999). *The Big Box*. New York: Hyperion Books for Children.

Robertson, B. (1999). *Marguerite Makes a Book*. Los Angeles: J. Paul Getty Museum.

Simon, C. (1999). *I Like to Win!* Brookfield, CT: The Millbrook Press.

Vaughan, M. (1999). *Abbie Against the Storm: The True Story of a Young Heroine and a Lighthouse*. Hillsboro, OR: Beyond Words Publishing, Inc.

Wallace, B. (1994). *The Biggest Klutz in the Fifth Grade*. New York: Minstrel Books.

CHAPTER 2

My Family

CARING CIRCLE

My Family

The family is the nucleus of civilization.
—Will and Ariel Durant

The Concept of Family

The family as the nucleus of society is a dynamic force—changing as the world changes—viewed through a broad spectrum of manifestations with influences that extend beyond the immediate kinship. Within the last century, the concept of family has transformed dramatically as society has moved from the industrial age to the information age. In the past, the nuclear family was static consisting of mother, father, children, and other close relatives living in close proximity. Today the nuclear family is more fluid—composed of one adult and child/children or may be extended to include adults, children, and other relatives in some form of kinship. The affiliation among members may change over time.

The Role of Caring in the Family

Despite the diversity in size and composition of a family, there is a sense of oneness in a family. Much like a mosaic, various parts connect to reveal a picture of closeness and caring. This loving connection emerges by the sharing of feelings and responsibilities toward one another. Family members provide a strong support unit in a holistic relationship that enhances physical, emotional, social, and spiritual development.

Taking Family Action

A concerted effort must be made by family and extended family members to ensure that the holistic relationship takes place through love. It is demonstrated by family members accepting each other as they are by listening, sharing, and giving wholeheartedly to one another. Family members share joy and sorrows while working together to defend and protect members against adversity as well as participate in family activities.

CARING CONNECTIONS

26 Fairmount Avenue

The Connection: *26 Fairmount Avenue* by Tomie dePaola, 1999
Genre: Nonfiction, Chapter Book
Level: Bridge
Reader: Teacher & Student
The Book: Award-winning illustrator/author, dePaola, shared the memories of a period in his life during the late 1930s. In this sensitive, humorous, nostalgic look, the readers are introduced to his family—mom, dad, and brother Buddy and his extended family including Nanas, grandpa Tom, and assorted aunts and uncles. The story dealt with the year the family faced the trials of having their new house built on 26 Fairmount Avenue. Frustrated by obstacles such as the hurricane of 1938, mudslides, and grassfires, Tomie related how his family coped throughout this construction project. The one joy Tomie experienced was painting pictures of his family on the bare walls of the new house, thus discovering his natural talent that would forecast his future profession as an illustrator. The year ended happily as the family finally moved into 26 Fairmont Avenue.

Human Rights Article(s):
> Article 13: Right to free movement in and out of the country
> Article 17: The right to own property

NCSS Standard(s):
> II. Time, Continuity, and Change
> III. People, Places, and Environments

Knowledge:
- Recall important family-related memories mentioned by Tomie.
- Describe feelings expressed about these family-related memories.
- Recall important personal family-related memories and describe feelings about them.
- Relate person memories to those written by Tomie.

Skills:
- Using *26 Fairmont Avenue* as a model, organize personal memories like chapters in a book.
- Classify the Tomie's and personal memories according to feelings.
- Determine how remembrances are influenced by events, family structure, and the home in which one lives.
- Gather home design data from magazines and Internet searches.

- Predict logical floor plan for a home that would fit the needs of personal family.
- In small groups, express the reasons why the floor plan is the best possible for each individual.

Value(s): Family experiences become cherished memories throughout life.

Activities: I = Individual   P = Partners   G = Group

A. Memory Gallery (G, I)

Materials: butcher paper, construction paper, markers, crayons, paint media, white glue, rulers, scissors, black tape

After reading *26 Fairmont Avenue*, students list Tomie's family memories. In like manner, students identify and list their own family memories for the past two years. Relate Tomie's family memories to personal family memories. Students organize their own remembrances in sequential order by event. Have students chose the eight most memorable events to represent in chronological order on a remembrance timeline. Give each student a piece of butcher paper (size determined by available space in the classroom) to illustrate timeline and memories. Draw timeline and hash marks using black tape on the paper. Students create eight picture frames out of construction paper and glue four frames on each side of the timeline. Students create pictures of memorable family events and record them sequentially within the frames. Wallpaper the classroom in gallery fashion with the illustrated timelines.

Questions to Ask:
1. What memorable events occurred in the book according to Tomie?
2. According to your recollections what memorable events occurred with you and your family?
3. How do your memories compare to Tomie's?
4. What factors did you use to select the events portrayed on your timeline?
5. How were your selections influenced by events, family members, and/or the home in which you live?

B. Stormy Weather Memory (I, P)

Materials: shoebox, index paper, construction paper, scissors, white glue, crayons, markers, miniature furniture, and other realistic materials (optional)

Have students identify a stormy weather event during which their family was together. Each student should construct a mental map on paper in web form depicting the storm in symbols, words, and pictures. Using a shoebox and the other materials, students depict the storm that was experienced by the family in a diorama. Label the project based on the type of storm that was experienced. In partners, the students share their family stormy weather remembrances. Display dioramas throughout the classroom for all to view and discuss.

C. Constructing Memories (I)

Materials: graph paper, rulers, pencils, markers, crayons, magazines (i.e., *Better Homes and Gardens*), Internet search (i.e., homeandgarden.com)

Students should discuss with their immediate family members family memories, needs, and wishes that are related to the structure, size, and layout of their home. Record family memories, needs, and wishes in a journal or notebook for future reference. In a class group, children may discuss the results of their family wish lists. In pairs, students peruse magazines and Internet sites that show room and home design. Discuss preferences and determine which ideas best fits the wish lists of their own families based on notes from the family meetings. Using graph paper and other materials, students individually design their own floor plan and front view of their ideal home. Based on wish lists, students should write a paragraph explaining how their decisions/designs were influenced. Have students share floor plans and rationale with the class, then take their designs home to share with their families.

Families

The Connection: *Families* by Meredith Tax, 1996
Genre: Picture Storybook
Level: Primary
Reader: Teacher
The Book: A look at various types of families through the perspective of six-year old Angie is told in delightful detail. Angie described her own family and her friends' families by making comparisons to animal as well as human families. She detailed the number of parents, where they lived, family size, and unique characteristics of each family group including single parent, divorced, traditional, same gender, and adoptive parents. As one of her classmates had no father, Angie and her friends decided to become her family. The important feature noted in the story was that love should be the tie that binds families together.

Human Rights Article(s):

      Article 16:   Right to marriage and family

      Article 12:   Freedom from interference with privacy, family, home, and correspondence

NCSS Standard(s):

  I. Culture

 V. Individuals, Groups, and Institutions

Knowledge:

- Identify similarities between Angie's family and various types of families.
- Identify the unique differences between Angie's family and other families.
- Explain how love connects all kinds of families.

Skills:

- Investigate the various families, homes, activities, and responsibilities described in *Families*.
- Summarize family information that was gathered into categories of family members, types of homes, and family activities and responsibilities.
- Students compare a family as described in the book and on the chart to their personal family.
- Express how the feelings between family members as described in the book show love and then how the feelings shared among personal family members support the notion of love.

Value(s): Love is the tie that connects members of a family together.

Activities: I = Individual   P = Partners   G = Group

A. Family Facts: Angie and Her Friends (G)

Materials: chart paper, markers, "Families" reproducible

Students listen for the various family members for each family mentioned as the teacher reads aloud from *Families*. Following the story, students will identify Angie's family and name the members and family activities and responsibilities. Then, other families from the book will be identified in the same manner. Following this discussion, information will be recorded in pictures and words on chart paper. (See reproducible.) Once all of the information has been gatheed on the chart, students will draw conclusions based on the following questions.

Figure 2.1

Families

	Angie	George	Marisol	Louie	Douglas	Willie	Susie	My Own Family
Members	Mother Father Step-Mother							
Home								
Activities	ZOO							

Questions to Ask:

1. How is Angie's family like the other families? How is her family different? How is George's family different from Douglas's and Willie's? How is Louie's family different from all of the other families.
2. Which family is most like your family? Explain.
3. We know what kind of homes Angie, Marisol, and Douglas live in. What do you think the homes of George, Willie, Louie, and Susie are like? Tell us about your home. How is your home like or different from the ones in the story?
4. What did the children in the book do for fun? What do you do for fun? How are your activities like the ones the children did in the book?
5. What kinds of things did the grown-ups do? What kinds of things do the grown-ups do in your family?
6. What kinds of activities can all family members do together?

The chart should be posted in an area of the classroom so that all students can view it. The information can support many activities that emphasize family ties.

B. My Family Scrap Book (I, P)

Materials: index paper, metal rings, construction paper, one-hole punch, glue, crayons, scissors

The teacher will send a letter explaining the project to parent(s) and/or guardian(s). The adults in each family will have a role to play in helping the children gather pictures and other materials for inclusion in the scrapbook. Their help will be necessary for identifying and arranging the

My Family Scrapbook

materials. (It may be helpful for the teacher to scan or duplicate the pictures so that the originals may be returned.) In class, students will compile their scrapbooks by making a cover, framing their photos and other materials with construction paper, and drawing activities and designs as enhancements. Using a one-hole punch, make a hole in the corner through all pages. Secure the scrapbook pages with the metal ring. Students take the scrapbooks home to work with adults to label people and activities. The completed scrapbooks may be shared with classmates, then displayed throughout the classroom.

C. LoveMobile (P)

Materials: construction paper, scissors, large heart pattern, small heart pattern, white glue or glue stick, decorative string, stapler, crayons and/or markers

After reading or listening to *Families*, the children will formulate "verbs" that depict loving behaviors among family members. It might be helpful to hold a discussion about the kinds of activities in which families engage, then compile behavior words (helping, caring, trusting, giving, etc.), with guidance, on a chart so that children may use them as helpful references. In pairs, children discuss ways in which they show love in their own families, then agree on four or five words that best fit their own family relationships. Using the small heart

LoveMobile

pattern, trace four or five hearts on construction paper. Write one of the chosen loving behavior words on each heart. Using the large heart pattern, trace two hearts on construction paper. Each member of the working pairs should draw and color a picture of their own immediate family, including all members. Cut out and glue the pictures on each large heart. Glue the large hearts from each working pair together with the family picture side out. Staple a three-foot length of decorative string to the center-top of each large heart. Staple one-foot lengths of decorative string to the center-tops of each of the small hearts, then attach to the bottom of the large heart so that it is balanced. Hang the *LoveMobiles* around the room as reminders of the loving relationships in which families may engage. Have each working pair describe how they chose their loving words. Each individual should plan one way to show the family that love is the tie that binds families together.

Magic Windows/Ventanas Mágicas
and
A Piece of My Heart/Pedacito de mi Corazón

Note to the Reader: The young reader's understanding of life in a Mexican American family is enhanced by the concept of family as perceived by the author/artist, Carmen Lomas Garza through the illustrations and information contained in these two books. The NCSS Standards, the Human Rights Articles, and activities included here pertain to both books.

The Connection: *Magic Windows/Ventanas Mágicas* by Carmen Lomas Garza, 1999
    Genre: Artistic Biography and Cultural History
    Level: Intermediate
    Reader: Student

The Book: Using the traditional folk art form of cut-paper, *papel picado,* Garza provided a window of discovery into her family, culture, and history. She framed snapshots of her life in cut-paper art that was taught to her by her grandmother. These unique pictures tied Aztec culture and Mexican traditions to the activities in her family life. The artist depicted the role of her grandfather growing plants in the garden by showing him cutting cactus and watering corn. She spoke of her close relationship with her grandparents and the family activities in which they engaged. The role of animals in culture and in legend was displayed in several of the boldly colored pages. The last window showed the artist teaching her niece and nephews how to make *papel picado,* connecting the children to their past.

The Connection: *A Piece of My Heart/Pedacito de mi Corazón* by Carmen Lomas Garza, 1991
    Genre: Nonfiction, Picture Book
    Level: Intermediate
    Reader: Teacher

The Book: Lomas used her artistic talent to portray her reminisces of Chicano family life and culture in a Texas barrio. Through paintings, prints, paper cutouts, and triptychs, the artist shared her experiences of the *familia* to enhance an understanding of Chicano culture. The extended family gathered food, cooked meals, and vacationed together. The importance of religion in their lives was shown in such paintings as *Posada, Cascarones,* and *El Milagro.* The families also participated in community fairs as depicted in *La Feria en Reynosa* and *Cakewalk.* The family tradition of storytelling was sketched with great sensitivity in the 1989 gouache, *La Llorona.* Through her artwork, Garza truly represented the love and caring cohesiveness of the Chicano family.

Human Rights Article(s):

Article 16:   Right to marriage and family

Article 18:   Freedom of belief and religion

Article 27:   Right to participate in the cultural life of community

NCSS Standard(s):

I. Culture

V. Individuals, Groups, and Institutions

IV. Individual Development and Identity

Knowledge:

- Identify traditions practiced in Garza's Mexican American family.
- Describe the family relationships depicted in *Magic Windows.*
- Explain how traditions influence relationships in Garza's Mexican American family.
- Recall personal family traditions.

Skills:

- Find information about family traditions and practices of a Chicano family in a Texas barrio.
- Gather information about personal family traditions and practices.
- Draw conclusions about relationships based on comparisons between personal family traditions and practices to those of Garza.
- Formulate a new family tradition that could enhance caring family relationships.

Value(s): Family practices and cultural traditions strengthen caring family relationships.

Activities: I = Individual   P = Partners   G = Group

A. Traditions Web (G, I)

Materials: paper, pencil, pens, both books, overhead projector, transparencies with markers

After students read *Magic Windows*, the teacher shares the art and information from *A Piece of My Heart*. Using both of these books as references, the students and teacher develop a concept web that portrays the traditions presented in the books. The topic could be Garza's Traditions with the four subtopics of Food, Art, Dance, and Celebrations. Students contribute details for the subtopics as the teacher records information in web form on the transparency. Using the same four subtopics, individually, students think about their personal families to create their own *Traditions Webs*. Once students complete their own webs, reconvene the class to answer questions about Garza's and their own traditions.

Questions to Ask:
1. What traditions were practiced in Garza's family?
2. What traditions are practiced in your own family?
3. How do your personal traditions compare to Garza's family traditions?
4. How do these traditions reinforce caring relations among families?
5. What tradition in your own family seems to promote the most caring feeling among family members? Explain.

Students should save their *Traditions Webs* in their journals or notebooks for future reference.

B. Caring Flowery Speech (P, I)

Materials: 14 x 17 white construction paper, 8½ x 11 black construction paper, scissors, white glue, watercolor markers, glitter glue, easel, pages 28 and 29 in *Magic Windows*, projector

Discuss the tradition of flowery speech with the students sharing the illustration in Garza's book. Students will be creating their own flowery speech images incorporating caring words that relate to family traditions. First, have students develop individual lists of caring family tradition words. Students save their lists for future use in the *Caring Flowery Speech* project. Using any projector with a light source, students in pairs cast a shadow on their partner to create a silhouette on the black construction paper. Typically, the easiest method is to have one child sit in a chair in profile with the black paper taped to the wall or chalkboard and the projector shining on the opposite side. The partner carefully traces, in full detail, the shadow cast on the black construction paper. Students cut out their own silhouettes and glue them to a corner of the white construction paper. Once this is completed, they are ready to draw the plant as shown in the book. They should keep in mind that the number of flowers on the plant will match the number of caring words created. Using the watercolor markers, the plant and flowers can come to life. In the center of each flower, students write a caring word and trace the letters with glitter glue. Students create speeches about their works of art, remembering to include family traditions and the concept of caring. When they individually present, the *Caring Flowery Speech* artwork is displayed on an easel.

D. Creating Family Traditions (P)

Materials: paper, pencils, camcorder, videotape

Using individual *tradition webs*, children in three to four member groups share their family traditions. Group members are responsible for gathering information about family and cultural traditions using a variety of sources (i.e., Internet, books, surveys). When reporting the information to partners, one member, as recorder, keeps a record of the traditions presented. Based on the information presented, students discuss the criteria involved in a family tradition (i.e., usual practice, something passed down from one generation to another, includes family members, etc.). Students then speculate on possible new traditions that could meet these criteria. In each partners group, students brainstorm ideas for a new family tradition. Evaluation of the brainstormed ideas includes: Could it be done? Does it meet all members' family needs and interests? Is it affordable? Can it be repeated on a regular basis? Having evaluated each idea, partners must come to consensus on one family tradition. Students name the tradition, identify a purpose, explain how it is implemented (when it will occur, where it will take place, what activities will be included), and describe why the families will accept this as a tradition. Partners plan a role-playing vignette of the newly created family tradition. They assign roles and practice for videotaping. In a secluded area, partners set the scene with props and videotape the occasion. The videotapes are presented during family tradition day in class, with family members as invited guests.

Bud, not Buddy

The Connection: *Bud, not Buddy* by Christopher Paul Curtis, 1999.
Genre: Historical Fiction, Chapter Book
Level: Intermediate
Reader: Teacher & Student
The Book: Undaunted by the depression, Bud, at ten years of age, searched for his family ties. His journey took him to the abusive Amos foster family, the Flint library, "Hooverville" via Flint, Michigan, The Dusky Devastators of the Depression band, and Grand Calloway Station. His street-wise "rules to have a funner life and make a better liar out of yourself" served to support him during times that would make grown men cringe and hide. This serious, yet lighthearted novel told the story of Bud who, at six years of age, lost his

mother and completed the family connection when he found his grandfather four years later. The historical references to the Depression, unions, and segregation added a special dimension to this family tale.

Human Rights Article(s):
> Article 3: Right to life, liberty, and personal security
>
> Article 25: Right to an adequate living standard

NCSS Standard(s):
  I Culture
 II. Time, Continuity, and Change
III. Individual Development and Identity

Knowledge:
- Identify ways in which life differed for families during the Depression.
- Describe Bud's life within the environment produced by the Depression.
- Cite the factors that helped Bud cope with the difficulties that he encountered.
- Elaborate on Bud's longing for family ties and his feelings of joy and grief when he finally connects with his grandfather.

Skills:
- Gather information concerning the conditions in the United States during the Depression.
- Compare how different families lived under these conditions.
- Relate family conditions during the depression to conditions today.
- Based on "Bud's rules" develop a set of rules for living in one's own personal/ family environment.
- Construct an artifact box that contains emotional connections with family.

Value(s): The family forms the core of one's spirit.

Activities: I = Individual   P = Partners   G = Group

A. Story Tree (G)

Materials: chart paper, markers, the book

After reading *Bud, not Buddy*, the class and teacher summarize setting (places where events occurred), characters (people involved in the events), and plot (the major events) in a tree organizer. The class may include places like Hooverville and the road between Flint and Grand

Rapids, people such as Todd Amos, Bugs, Herman E. Calloway, and situations like the cold walk on the road to Grand Rapids, the overnight stay in the Amos's shed among others. Once the Story Tree is complete, conduct a group discussion using the following questions.

Questions to Ask:
1. How did life during the Depression differ for the various families identified in the book?
2. How would you characterize Bud's life?
3. What events influenced Bud's ability to cope with being poor, having no family, and living in foster situations?
4. What feelings did Bud experience during his many setbacks and successes?
5. How is family life different today?

B. A Code for Coping: Rules for Living (I)

Materials: parchment paper, computer, color printer

Using the personal experiences and lessons learned from family members, students create their own rules for living that will provide a framework on which to make decisions independently.

C. Artifact Case (I)

Materials: shoebox, materials for covering boxes (wallpaper, newspaper, contact paper, etc.), important personal family-related objects

Students create an artifact case, much like Bud's suitcase, to reinforce family identity. The children make a list of objects they have collected and treasures that tie them to their family members. Gather and evaluate the artifacts in terms of reinforcing family identity and belonging for inclusion in the artifact case. Using the shoebox and materials for covering, select an appropriate material and cover the inside and outside of the box and cover. Place the selected artifacts into the box and keep in a safe place. Students should tell their family story to the class using the artifacts.

Luka's Quilt

The Connection: *Luka's Quilt* by Georgia Guback, 1994
Genre: Picture Story Book
Level: Primary, Bridge
Reader: Teacher & Student
The Book: Luka learned that compromise can be an important part of family harmony. Her grandmother made a traditional, two-color Hawaiian quilt for Luka's bed. Expecting a

multicolor floral quilt, Luka was disappointed and angry with her grandmother when she saw the finished green-and-white quilt. This situation lasted until the Lei Day celebration when grandmother suggested a truce. They went to the park where Luka participated in making a colorful lei. Tutu used the Luka's colorful lei as a model to sew a quilted replica. Sometimes Luka laid the colorful quilted lei on her green-and-white quilt, and sometimes she appreciated the traditional two colors. Now she could have it both ways, and Tutu and Luka were friends again.

Human Rights Article(s):
> Article 19: Freedom of opinion and information
> Article 27: Right to participate in the cultural life of community

NCSS Standard(s):
> I. Culture
> IV. Individual Development and Identity
> V. Individuals, Groups, and Institutions

Knowledge:
- Identify traditions of the Hawaiian culture as presented in *Luka's Quilt*.
- Describe the traditional Hawaiian quilt and the significance of using only two colors.
- Describe the practice of making flower leis.
- Explain the feelings of frustration and anger that arise between Luka and her grandmother related to the conflict of opinion and tradition.
- Relate how compromise leads to understanding.

Skills
- Investigate quilt designs of Hawaiian and other culture groups.
- Compare design and color of quilts between the Hawaiian culture and that of another culture.
- Create an original design for a quilt that reflects a collaborative effort based on students' cultural traditions.

Value(s): Compromise leads to resolution of conflict and respect for the opinions of others.

Activities: I = Individual   P = Partners   G = Group

A. Hawaiian Culture Lei (P, G)

Materials: flower pattern, pencils, bright-colored construction paper, glue sticks, markers, poster board, scissors

In partner groups of three members each, children are assigned a culture category (i.e., plants, animals, clothing, food, traditions, artifacts). Using *Luka's Quilt*, the library, and computer resources, children find out and record information about their category. In each partner group, the children choose the three best examples of their culture category. Each member then traces a flower onto the assigned colored construction paper and cuts it out. Record one example on each flower so that the partner group contributes three different culture flowers to the lei. A large circle is drawn on the poster board. Partner groups place their flowers onto the circle using glue sticks to complete the culture lei. Title the poster board and ask the following questions.

Questions to Ask:

1. What ideas about Hawaiian life are presented on the culture lei?
2. What would you choose as your favorite idea from the culture lei? Explain.
3. Which ideas that are listed on our culture lei are also found in *Luka's Quilt*?
4. According to the book, how many colors are used in traditional Hawaiian quilts? How does Luka feel about this practice?
5. How do you feel about the two-color quilt? How many colors do you think a quilt should have? Explain.

B. Peaceable Solutions (P)

Materials: lined chart paper (one sheet per partner group), markers, computer, paper

Form heterogeneous partner groups of three to four members. Ask group members to come to consensus about guidelines for working together. Students first brainstorm ideas (i.e., talk in quiet voices, all participate, be responsible for group work, respect the ideas and opinions of others, etc.) and record them on the chart paper. After reviewing the ideas, students choose the responses that will best support their working partner groups. The teacher reads a group problem scenario (similar to the example given) to the entire class. Students demonstrate how their peaceable solutions help to avoid conflict and support compromise.

When a partner group was working together to brainstorm a list of ideas, one member, who rarely spoke in a group, offered a suggestion. One other partner laughed at the idea and made this group member feel badly. What should the other partners do?

Students check their peaceable solutions to determine whether these solutions will guide them in resolving the conflict scenario. Teacher may present four or five different scenarios against which students check their lists of solutions. Then, on returning to partner groups, students revise their peaceable solutions. Prepare final "Peaceable Solutions" list and create a scroll-like document on the computer. Print and laminate the list. Students keep the finalized document in the permanent partner group folder for reference when working together.

C. Compromise Culture Quilt (P, G)

Materials: muslin squares, bright colored fabric, batting, thread, a variety of fabric markers and crayons, yarn, large-eye needle for yarn, paper, pencils

In partner groups, students share how their cultural background influences the celebration of special holidays. Each partner chooses one special holiday and draws a scene depicting the family celebration and describes the details to the group. The partner groups determine a common thread in each picture (i.e., contains family members). Then, the partners in each group come to agreement about a creative way to connect the pictures by drawing the same object in each one (i.e., a sun, food, flowers, buildings) and choosing coordinating colors (i.e., earth tones, two-tones). Students add the objects and coordinating colors to their individual pictures and return to the partner groups to come to consensus on the design and colors. Using fabric markers and crayons, students transfer their drawings onto the muslin squares. In the full-class setting, students come to consensus on the arrangement of the quilt squares for final stitching. Family volunteers stitch the prearranged squares together. The colorful material should be stitched around the squares as a border. Batting and backing is cut to fit the size of the quilt, and the edges are stitched. Using the yarn and yarn needles, students (in quilting bee fashion) stitch and tie yarn tufts in regular intervals to hold the batting in place. Once the Compromise Culture Quilt is completed, students may invite family members to come to a presentation of the class project.

The Silence in the Mountains

The Connection: *The Silence in the Mountains* by Liz Rosenberg, 1999

Genre: Picture Storybook

Level: Bridge

Reader: Student

The Book: When war broke out in Lebanon, the peaceful mountain life of Iskander and his family ended. The family gathered a few precious mementos and flew to safety in America. The noise of the city made Iskander long for the silence of the mountains he left back home. Later the family moved to a dairy farm in the hilly countryside. Iskander still felt that something was missing. His family tried to make him feel at home by giving a variety of activities to complete. It was not until his grandfather took him up deep into the woods that Iskander discovered a new silence, different from the past, but still good.

Human Rights Article(s):

> Article 3:   Right to life, liberty, personal security
>
> Article 13:   Right to free movement in and out of the country

NCSS Standard(s):

> III. People, Places, and Environments
>
> V. Individuals, Groups, and Institutions

Knowledge:

- Describe Iskander's native land.
- Identify features of Iskander's adopted land (both urban and rural)
- Compare the feelings Iskander held about his new home to those he felt about his former home in the mountains.
- Describe personal feelings about moving to a new home or locale.
- Compare personal feelings to Iskander's feelings about moving.

Skills:

- Collect information from friends, relatives, teachers, and so on about moving and the associated feelings.
- Analyze changes that come about in life and determine ways in which families cope.
- Present a vignette of stories about moving to the class.
- Come to consensus about endearing qualities of home.

Value(s): Loving family members provide security during life transitions.

Activities: I = Individual   P = Partners   G = Group

A. Relocation Recollections (I, G)

Materials: note pad, pencils, tape recorder (optional)

Individually, students find another person who has moved to interview. Using the following five questions, the students record information either on paper or tape.

1. What was the hardest thing about moving?
2. What was best thing about moving?
3. How is your new home like your old home?
4. How is it different?
5. What helped you feel better about moving to a new place?

Report the moving stories to the class. After reading the book, the teacher leads a discussion ased on the following questions.

Questions to Ask:
1. What was Iskander's native land like? What is Iskander's new land like?
2. What were Iskander's feelings about moving to his new home in the country?
3. How were Iskander's feelings about moving similar to those who you interviewed?
4. Who helped Iskander feel better about his new home?
5. Who helped others who have moved feel better?

B. Moving Memories (I)

Materials: "Moving Memories" reproducible, crayons, markers

Children determine the most moving information about moving and create a sequenced storyboard of events. They may use personal information or ideas gathered from others who have moved to create the illustrations. On the "Moving Memories Van" students reproduce the storyboards in vivid color. Each picture is labeled, and word balloons are added to refine the story. After the moving memories are presented to the class, students should determine common feelings and the related outcomes about moving. A brief description of how family members helped to ease the difficulties should be included.

C. Picture This (P)

Materials: digital camera, computer, printer, photo paper, three-ring binder

In partner groups of three to four members, students decide what features of their local area they would miss if they were to leave for a new area. Several images depicting these scenes are recorded using the digital camera (any camera may be used as long as images can be recorded on a computer disk). On a computer, partner groups organize the digital images into a collage of "best things" and write a brief rationale for choosing these particular features. Print the photo collage with written rationale on photo paper and place in three-ring binder. Label the binder with "Picture This: What We Love About Our Area." As the year progresses new photos may be added, then compared to other places studied.

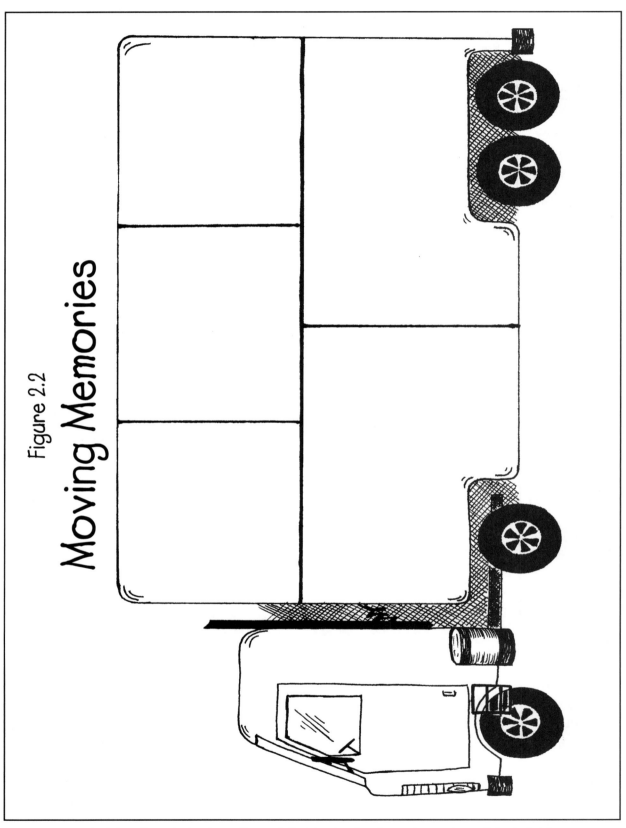

Figure 2.2
Moving Memories

CARING CORNER

Grandmother's Song

The Connection: *Grandmother's Song* by Barbara Soros, 1998
Genre: Picture Storybook
Level: Bridge, Intermediate
Reader: Teacher & Student
The Book: A Mexican grandmother taught her granddaughter how to face her fears by providing a loving, supporting environment. As the trembling granddaughter experienced anxious moments throughout her childhood, her grandmother held her, sang to her, stroked her, and passed on the wisdom of her matriarchal ancestors. The granddaughter learned the virtues of trusting, giving, and gentleness that she passed on to her own children. When the grandmother grew more frail, the granddaughter took loving care of her. The granddaughter was grief stricken when her grandmother died, but the spirit of her grandmother gave her the strength to carry on. Throughout the rest of her life, her grandmother was always with her.

Human Rights Article(s):

Article 3: Right to live, liberty, personal security
Article 18: Freedom of belief and religion
Article 27: Right to participate in the cultural life of community

NCSS Standard(s):

I. Culture
II. Time, Continuity, and Change
VI. Individual Development and Identity

Bess's Log Cabin Quilt

The Connection: *Bess's Log Cabin Quilt* by D. Anne Love, 1995
Genre: Historical Fiction, Chapter Book
Level: Intermediate
Reader: Student
The Book: While Bess's father was working on the Oregon Trail, life at the family farm took a turn for the worse. Bess's mother took ill with "swamp fever," her father's return was delayed and he was feared dead, and they were threatened with the loss of their farm if they failed to pay the local usurer 100 dollars. Bess remembered that a big monetary prize was offered for the best quilt at the fair. While taking care of her mother and tending the farm, Bess worked night and day on her quilt in hopes of winning enough money to resolve the

family's debt problem. When she got to the fair and saw the other quilts that had been entered into the contest, she realized that she would be very lucky to win any prize. A family friend, who took great pride in winning each year, withdrew her remarkable quilt from the contest so that Bess won a prize. When Bess returned home, a bigger prize awaited her; father had returned.

Human Rights Article(s):
Article 12:   Freedom from interference with privacy, family, home and correspondence
Article 17:   Right to own property

NCSS Standard(s):
II.   Time, Continuity, and Change
VII. Individual Development and Identity

Something from Nothing

The Connection: *Something from Nothing* by Phoebe Gilman, 1992
Genre: Folktale, Picture Storybook
Level: Primary
Reader: Teacher & Student
The Book: In this delightful Jewish folktale, Joseph's grandfather, a tailor, made a blanket for him to keep him warm and safe. Throughout Joseph's childhood, his grandfather recycled the blanket into a jacket, a vest, a tie, a handkerchief, and a button. Finally, the button was lost, and his grandfather agreed that he couldn't make "something from nothing." However, in school, Joseph had just enough material to make a story.

Human Rights Article(s):
Article 3:   Right to life, liberty, personal security
Article 19: Freedom of opinion and information

NCSS Standard(s):
I.   Culture
IV. Individual Development and Identity

Luba and the Wren

The Connection: *Luba and the Wren* by Patricia Polacco, 1999
Genre: Picture Storybook
Level: Primary, Bridge
Reader: Teacher & Student

The Book: While walking in the forest, Luba, a young Russian girl, freed a captured bird. For her kind gesture, the wren granted Luba a wish that she declined. Returning to her broken-down *dacha*, her poor parents demanded that Luba ask the wren for a bigger house. Their wish was granted, but it failed to satisfy them for long. The embarrassed Luba was sent back to the wren several times that resulted in her parents becoming the emperor and empress of the world. When the discontented parents asked to be gods, the frustrated wren retaliated. Luba found herself back at the *dacha* with her parents who were now content with their real treasure, Luba.

Human Rights Article(s):

Article 3: Right to life, liberty, and personal security

NCSS Standard(s):

I. Culture

V. Individual Development and Identity

A Carp for Kimiko

The Connection: *A Carp for Kimiko* by Virginia Kroll, 1993

Genre: Picture Storybook

Level: Primary

Reader: Teacher

The Book: In Kimiko's family, it was traditional that only the boys were allowed to have kites on Children's Day. Kimiko longed to participate with her brothers on this Japanese holiday. Each brother had a carp kite to fly on this special day. To help Kimiko's cope, her mother told her that she could participate in the Doll Festival, a tradition for girls. Although disappointed, Kimiko still enjoyed watching her brothers participate in the Children's Day celebration. The next morning, a happy Kimiko was presented a real carp by her mother and father.

Human Rights Article(s):

Article 1: Right to equality

Article 2: Freedom from discrimination

Article 27: Right to participate in the cultural life of community

NCSS Standard(s):

I. Culture

IV. Individual Development and Identity

Shades of Gray

The Connection: *Shades of Gray* by Carolyn Reeder, 1999.

Genre: Historical Fiction, Chapter Book

Level: Intermediate

Reader: Student

The Book: Twelve-year old Will Page was left an orphan after the Civil War and was sent, unwillingly, to live on a farm with his Uncle Jed and Aunt Ella. Still grieving over the loss of his family, Will had difficulty adjusting because he was filled with resentment against his uncle who chose not to fight for the Confederacy. Will considered him a traitor and a coward, especially as his father and brother were killed by the Yankees. Working side-by-side with his uncle doing farm chores, Will came to realize that Jed was a brave man who had the courage to choose against war and killing. Although he had the opportunity to live with others, Will chose to stay with his new, caring family.

Human Rights Article(s):

Article 18: Freedom of belief and religion

NCSS Standard(s):

II. Time, Continuity, and Change

IV. Individual Development and Identity

V. Individuals, Groups, and Institutions

Edwurd Fudwupper Fibbed Big

The Connection: *Edwurd Fudwupper Fibbed Big* by Berkeley Breathed, 2000

Genre: Picture Storybook

Level: Bridge

Reader: Teacher & Student

The Book: Appealing to all ages, this humorous tale was written about an outstanding liar, Edwurd and his ignored little sister Fannie Fudwupper. His friends and neighbors were often the butt of his creative falsehoods. Edwurd told the greatest fib of all when he accidentally broke his mother's favorite ceramic pig. The results were catastrophic, bringing the army, air force, and even aliens from outer space to plague the neighborhood and the fibber himself. The care and concern of his little sister, Fannie, forced Edwurd to admit his guilt and left them both with a new spirit of togetherness.

Human Rights Article(s):

Article 3: Right to life, liberty, personal security

Article 11: Right to be considered innocent until proven guilty

NCSS Standard(s):

   IV. Individual Development and Identity

    V. Individuals, Groups, and Institutions

    X. Civic Ideals and Practices

In Daddy's Arms I Am Tall: African Americans Celebrating Fathers

The Connection: *In Daddy's Arms I Am Tall: African Americans Celebrating Fathers* by various African American poets, J. Steptoe, illustrator, 1997

Genre: Verse, Picture Book

Level: Bridge, Intermediate

Reader: Student

The Book: The unique, multitextured illustrations by Jevoka Steptoe captured the essence of the verse presented by eleven poets. The juxtaposition of the sensitive, meaningful poetry and the creative graphic art provided a significant tribute to all African American fathers and grandfathers. Children should be inspired by the love and caring that was evident between the men and their children.

Human Rights Article(s):

   Article 2: Freedom from discrimination

   Article 3: Right to life, liberty, personal security

  Article 16: Right to marriage and family

NCSS Standard(s):

    I. Culture

   IV. Individual Development and Identity

    V. Individuals, Groups, and Institutions

The Lamp, the Ice, and the Boat called Fish

The Connection: *The Lamp, the Ice, and the Boat Called Fish* by Jacqueline Briggs Martin, 2001

Genre: Historical Fiction, Chapter Book

Level: Intermediate

Reader: Student

The Book: The true story of the ill-fated journey of the Kurluk (Fish) and its passengers, who were eventually caught in a sea of ice, was graphically reported. Although the ship carried passengers such as the scientists of the Canadian Arctic Expedition, the story focused on an Inupiaq family, the parents and two young girls. Throughout the harrowing year as captives of the ice, their family spirit and a special seal oil lamp warmed and sustained them through the frigid cold, sickness, and near starvation until their rescue and safe arrival back home.

Human Rights Article(s):

Article 3: Right to life, liberty, personal security

NCSS Standard(s):

I. Culture

II. Time, Continuity, and Change

V. Individuals, Groups, and Institutions

A Golden Age

The Connection: *A Golden Age* by Martha Wickham, 1996

Genre: Historical Fiction, Picture Storybook

Level: Intermediate

Reader: Student

The Book: While visiting at the Information Age Exhibit at the National Museum of American History Emma was placed in a time warp situation when she saw an old radio like the one her grandmother kept in her living room. She found herself not only back in 1945, but she also had become her own grandmother, Emelia. Shocked to find no TV present, she discovered that her family enjoyed listening to the radio. Her grandparents listened to the news, soap operas, nighttime dramas, and even danced to the music of the big bands. But mostly, the family was overjoyed and relieved to hear the announcement that the war in Germany had ended. Back to the present, Emma now understood why Grandmother still kept her radio.

Human Rights Article(s):

Article 3: Right to life, liberty, personal security

Article 24: Right to rest and leisure

NCSS Standard(s):

I. Culture

II. Time, Continuity, and Change

IV. Individual Development and Identity

The Journey

The Connection: *The Journey* by Sarah Stewart, 2001

Genre: Picture Storybook

Level: Intermediate

Reader: Student

The Book: Since her Aunt Sarah gave up her place to Hannah for her birthday present, the young Amish girl left her farm home for a short visit to the big city. Hannah wrote in a diary of her adventures and feelings about her stay. Although she was excited and happy to view the tall buildings, art museum, aquarium, and cathedral, and to buy a hot dog from a street vendor, each venue brought back an image of life back at the farm. After a week, she was glad to be home, for she had missed everyone, even her brothers!

Human Rights Article(s):

Article 2: Freedom from discrimination

Article 18: Freedom of belief and religion

NCSS Standard(s):

I. Culture

III. People, Places, and Environments

CARING COLLECTION: FAMILY

Breathed, B. (2000). *Edwurd Fudwupper Fibbed Big*. Boston: Little, Brown.

Curtis, C. P. (1999). *Bud, Not Buddy*. New York: Delacorte Press.

DePaola, T. (1999). *26 Fairmount Avenue*. New York: G. P. Putnam's Sons.

Garza, C. L. (1999). *Magic Windows/Ventanas Mágicas*. San Francisco: Children's Book Press.

———. (1991). *A Piece of My Heart/Pedacito de Mi Corazón*. New York: The New Press.

Gilman, P. (1992). *Something from Nothing*. New York: Scholastic.

Guback, G. (1994). *Luka's Quilt*. New York: Greenwillow Books.

Kroll, V. (1993). *A Carp for Kimiko*. Watertown, MA: Charlesbridge Publishing.

Love, D. A. (1995). *Bess's Log Cabin Quilt*. New York: Bantam Doubleday Dell Books for Young Readers.

Martin, J. B. (2001). *The Lamp, the Ice, and the Boat Called Fish*. New York: Houghton Mifflin.

Polacco, P. (1999). *Luba and the Wren*. New York: Penguin Putnam Books for Young Readers.

Reeder, C. (1991). *Shades of Gray*. New York: Avon Books.

Rosenberg, L. (1999). *The Silence in the Mountains*. New York: Orchard Books.

Soros, B. (1998). *Grandmother's Song*. New York: Barefoot Books.

Steptoe, J., illustrator. (1997). *In Daddy's Arms I Am Tall: African Americans Celebrating Fathers*. New York: Lee & Low Books.

Stewart, S. (2001). *The Journey*. New York: Farrar, Straus & Giroux.

Tax, M. (1996). *Families*. New York: The Feminist Press.

Wickham, M. (1996). *A Golden Age*. Washington, DC: The Smithsonian Institution.

CHAPTER 3

Our School

CARING CIRCLE

Our School

A school should not be a preparation for life.
A school should be life.
—Elbert Hubbard

The Concept of School

Throughout American history, the school has had the responsibility of passing on knowledge and skills to the youth of the nation. That role remains constant and significant in modern times but has expanded to include societal values that were traditionally taught in the family. The school environment should target those qualities reflected in life and esteemed by a democratic society. Some characteristics that are thought to be important, useful, and prized by people and taught in schools include, among others, honesty, justice, respect, responsibility, tolerance, co-operation, empathy, and caring.

The Role of Caring in the School

The first step is for faculty and staff to model the characteristics of caring for children to assimilate them into their own behaviors. The teaching of caring values is not an incidental, haphazard practice. Teaching content knowledge, skills, and values must be developed as an integrated process within a systematic caring curriculum and a nurturing climate across all levels and classrooms. Throughout the various content areas, when opportunities for promoting and nurturing caring actions arise teachers must be prepared to implement appropriate strategies.

Taking School Action

Students reflect on the content from a caring, empathetic perspective that finds expression in their words, gestures, and actions. They implement caring behaviors and attitudes by supporting one another in cognitive and social situations through collaboration. They show respect for other students, teachers, principal, and staff. Students are sensitive to the needs of others particularly to those who are intellectually, emotionally, and culturally diverse, and they are generous with their time and efforts to help meet those needs. In addition, there is an understanding that school property belongs to everyone, and all should share in the responsibility to care for it.

CARING CONNECTIONS

How to Be Cool in the Third Grade

The Connection: *How to Be Cool in the Third Grade* by Betsy Duffey, 1995
Genre: Fiction, Chapter Book
Level: Bridge
Reader: Student
The Book: Robert Hayes York wanted to start his first day in the third grade being cool. Keeping him from this goal were his clothes (superhero underwear and shorts instead of jeans), the nickname "Robbie" printed on his backpack, and his mom who not only walked him to the bus stop, but also kissed him in front of the bus riders. He decided on a strategy to overcome these obstacles to cool. Before doing so, he had to confront the third-grade bully, Bo, who had ways (e.g., calling him *Superwobbie*) to make his school days uncomfortable. When he found out he was to be Bo's book buddy, Rob became anxious. While working together, Rob discovered Bo's real name and suggested a possible nickname. An unspoken pledge developed that there would be no more hurtful nicknames from either side. Rob was cool, at last.

Human Rights Article(s):
   Article 3:   Right to life, liberty, personal security

NCSS Standard(s):
   IV.   Individual Development and Identity
   V.   Individuals, Groups, and Institutions

Knowledge:
   • Describe how a bully could create fear among the children on the bus and in school.
   • Identify the specific behaviors Bo displays toward Robbie.
   • Determine the similarities between Bo and Robbie that lead to the beginnings of a more caring relationship.
   • Identify behaviors that could build understanding between a bully and the rest of a class.

Skills:

- Using the book, search for information about the behaviors that were demonstrated by Bo.
- Reflect on the behaviors of bullies who have been observed or personally experienced.
- Categorize bullying behaviors into verbal and physical.
- Analyze the behaviors that brought Robbie and Bo together and construct ideas for creating caring relationships.

Value(s): All children must be safe from ridicule and physical assault among their peers in a school setting.

Activities: I = Individual   P = Partners   G = Group

A. Bully's Behavior (G)

Materials: chart paper, markers, the book

Using the book, have the children search for behaviors that Bo displays. Teacher divides the chart paper into two sections with space for a title at the top of each column (T-chart). Students classify Bo's behaviors as either verbal or physical as they are listed on the chart. Students reflect on their own experiences with bullies either as observer or victims and identify and classify them in the same manner. Teacher records responses and asks the following questions.

Questions to Ask:

1. According to the chart, what words might a bully use?
2. According to the chart, what actions might a bully take?
3. How did Robbie feel when he was the victim of a bully?
4. How would you feel if you were a victim of a bully?
5. Why do you think bullies act and talk as they do?
6. How did the situation with Robbie and Bo get resolved?

B. Robbie's Resolution (P)

Materials: cardboard squares, paper, crayons, markers, pencils, the book

In partner groups of three members each, children discuss all of the actions that Robbie took to avoid being picked on, the factors that brought about the final resolution, and the resolution itself. In planning a storyboard, each partner group sketches pictures on paper of what was discussed. Dialog balloons are added to the sketch to clarify the behaviors. Pictures are divided among partners so that all participate in creating the storyboard pictures and dialog balloons on the cardboard squares. Partners plan how to present their sequenced storyboards to the class. Partners display the storyboards on the chalk tray while presenting commentary about the behaviors that led to the resolution and a new caring relationship.

C. Nice Nicknames (P)

Materials: hangers, thread, one-hole punch, 5 x 8 index cards, markers, crayons, glitter glue, scissors

Like Bo, have the children create nicknames for themselves that they really like and symbolize who they are. On the index cards, students record their nicknames in bold, decorative style using markers, crayons, and glitter. Partners share with their team positive (nice) traits about each other. On the other side of the index card, each partner records their own positive traits suggested by the team. Students may want to use scissors to cut their nickname cards into interesting shapes. Punch a hole and tie a length of thread through each card. Attach the *Nice Nicknames* to a hanger above each partner group's desks for everyone to view.

The Brand New Kid

The Connection: *The Brand New Kid* by Katie Couric, 2000
Genre: Picture Storybook
Level: Primary
Reader: Student & Teacher
The Book: On their first day in second grade, Ellie and her friend Carrie discovered a new boy in class called Lazlo who just moved into the community. He looked, talked, and acted differently than the other students. Because of this, he was either ignored or picked on by his classmates. Coming to realize how unhappy this made Lazlo, Ellie spent some time at his house playing games. She told her friends that Lazlo was just like them and even had special talents. Lazlo was finally accepted by the group.

Human Rights Article(s):

Article 2: Freedom from discrimination

NCSS Standard(s):

I. Culture
IV. Individual Development and Identity
V. Individuals, Groups, and Institutions

Knowledge:
- Identify the feelings that Lazlo had as the new student in second grade.
- Describe how Lazlo was treated by the other children.
- Compare the feelings that Lazlo held to personal feelings when confronted with an unfamiliar situation and new people.
- Detail the resolution to your personal unfamiliar situation.
- Explain how Ellie got the other students to accept Lazlo.

Skills:
- Compare and contrast Lazlo's situation to your own.
- Summarize commonalties to both personal and Lazlo's unfamiliar situations.
- Analyze the behaviors that contributed to Lazlo's isolation and then later acceptance by the class.
- Create a classroom model that supports the integration of new students.

Value(s): All children should be appreciated for their unique qualities and accepted into the group.

Activities: I = Individual   P = Partners   G = Group

A. New and Blue (G)

Materials: chart paper, markers, the book

Divide the chart paper into two columns labeling the first "Lazlo's Feelings" and the second "Our Feelings." Review the book, *The Brand New Kid*, discussing the feelings that Lazlo had as a new kid in school. Record these feelings in the appropriate column on the chart. Discuss feelings that the children in class may have had when confronting new situations. Record these in "Our Feelings." Using the following questions and the *New and Blue* chart conduct a class discussion.

Questions to Ask:
1. How are Lazlo's feelings like your feelings?
2. How are they different?
3. What are the common characteristics in both situations?
4. What actions did the other children take that made Lazlo feel so blue?
5. What did Ellie do to make Lazlo feel better?
6. What could we do to make any new student feel better?

B. New Kid Caring Kit (P, G)

Materials: large plastic zipper bag, two-pocket school folder, paper and pencil, other appropriate materials as decided by the class

In partner groups of three students each, children collaborate to formulate a list of useful materials for a new student. Consideration should be given to cost and size of materials as well as student need and interest when determining items. For the zipper bag, items such as pencils, erasers, small rulers, treats, and so on could be considered. For the two-pocket folder, class lists, photos, calendar, student-created pictures, school map, and so forth may be important. Once the partner groups come to consensus on the important materials to be included in the *New Kid Caring Kit*, then they come together in the full-class group to discuss their ideas. Prioritize and determine which items will be included in the final kit that will be distributed to new children.

New Kid Caring Kit

C. New Kid Helping Booklet (P, G)

Materials: 8½ x 11 white paper, index stock, crayons, markers, pencils, stapler, computer, and scanner (optional)

The *New Kid Helping Booklet* should serve as a guide to the students for welcoming and including new people to the class. In a large group meeting, children decide the actions they could take to help the new person adjust to the new environment. Using Hilda Taba's Concept Attainment Model, the children then group their ideas based on similarities or patterns. Then the students label each group (e.g.. tour guide, mentor) and add anything that seems to be missing from the labeled groups. The labeled groups serve as subtopics for the booklet. Each partner group is assigned a subtopic to establish tasks and behaviors that should be carried out for that section. Using an 8½ x 11 sheet of paper placed in the landscape or horizontal position, fold vertically to form two booklet-sized pages. Each group records their formulated actions for the subtopic using both pictures and words. For those classrooms that have a computer and scanner, the text could be typed and the pictures scanned and arranged in a pleasing format. The teacher duplicates the students' work, places a colorful cover with title on the outside, and staples the spine. Copies should be distributed to all students and used when necessary. After a new student has been in the class for a month, have students interview that student to determine the effectiveness of the *New Kid Helping Booklet*. Make modifications as appropriate.

Dork in Disguise

The Connection:	*Dork in Disguise* by Carol Gorman, 1999
Genre:	Fiction, Chapter Book
Level:	Intermediate
Reader:	Student
The Book:	In an attempt to hide his ability and interest in school subjects that would

proclaim him a dork to his new sixth-grade classmates, Jerry Flack planned a course of action that would disguise him from old dork to new cool. This led him to lying about his past experiences, failing to care for classmates with similar interests, and joining a group that not only caused trouble in class, but also skipped school. Despite his acceptance by the cool group, Jerry could not resist joining his brainy friend, Brenda, on the science club team competition and working on his project, in secret. Jerry's work and success with his scientifically designed hovercraft brought about his realization that being smart is really cool.

Human Rights Article(s):

Article 2: Freedom from discrimination
Article 28: Right to social order assuring human rights

NCSS Standard(s):

IV. Individual Development and Identity
V. Individuals, Groups, and Institutions
X. Civic Ideals and Practices

Knowledge:

- Identify the various cliques in the book as well as in any school environment.
- Explain the feelings connected to being included in or left out of groups.

- Describe the problems and advantages that result from group identification.
- Reflect on your own feelings concerning belonging to a group or being isolated from others.

Skills:
- Gather data about the various cliques that exist in your own school, the feelings of members and nonmembers, and the lack of caring toward those outside the groups.
- Categorize the data according to positive, negative, or information-related impact to caring for others.
- Synthesize the information gathered into several scenarios for presentation using a problem-solving format for decision making.
- Determine the most relevant decisions to solve the problems.
- Construct strategies that would implement the decisions and result in caring actions.

Value(s): All children deserve to be valued and accepted.

Activities: I = Individual   P = Partners   G = Group

A. Cliques and Geeks (P)

Materials: computers, printer, pencil, paper, chart paper, markers, the book

Using the book as a guide, formulate questions for a survey about groups in the intermediate grades. Partner groups present the possible questions to the class. Teacher records those questions on chart paper so that students may review them and choose a few (10 or less) appropriate (clarity and relevance) open-ended items for a survey. Compile, duplicate, and distribute the survey to partner groups. During lunch, recess, and/or free time, group members gather data with the survey of other intermediate students. Using a "Pass-Around Chart," students in each partner group record comments from each question separately (one question per sheet) and pass it on until all data has been recorded. In a full-class meeting, students share the collected information.

Questions to Ask:
1. What are the different groups that exist in your school?
2. Why do members gather in the groups?
3. What common features exist within the groups?
4. What are the feelings of those who belong and those who do not belong?
5. What are the advantages or disadvantages that result from group identification?
6. How does group acceptance help or hinder caring relationships?

B. Scenarios for Caring Decision-Making (P, G)

Materials: "The Decision-Making Model" reproducible, paper, pencils

Using the reproducible, the teacher leads the class through the decision-making model (scenario, problem solving, and reflection). Partner groups create a scenario based on one of the groups/situations found in their surveys. The scenario should be an open-ended scene consisting of no fewer than three characters. One character is faced with making a decision that has possible positive or negative consequences. Each partner group presents a role-play of their scenario for the class. The class engages in the problem-solving and reflection process for each partner group scenario.

C. Schoolwide Caring Relationship Awareness (P, G)

Materials: scripts (partner-generated scenarios), "The Decision-Making Model" reproducible, chart paper, markers

The students will promote schoolwide caring relationships through presentations of the decision-making model in other classrooms. While the teacher records their comments, the class formulates an introduction that includes their purpose. All partner groups will use this introduction followed by a role-play presentation of their scenarios and the problem-solving process with reflection with their new audiences. After the presentations, partner groups distribute awareness cards that ask questions about the groups in school and how to promote caring relationships. Once collected and compiled, the responses may serve as an evaluation of student awareness of the importance of making caring decisions in the school setting.

Lilly's Purple Plastic Purse

The Connection: *Lilly's Purple Plastic Purse* by Kevin Henkes, 1996
Genre: Picture Storybook
Level: Primary
Reader: Teacher & Student
The Book: Lilly loved everything about school including her teacher, Mr. Slinger. She always followed the rules, participated in class, and was helpful by doing extra chores. One day Lilly brought her tuneful, purple, plastic purse and cool sunglasses to school. Not being able to wait until sharing time to show off her new persona, she interrupted the class and Mr. Slinger several times. As she was forced to give her prized possessions to her teacher for the rest of the day, an angry Lilly drew a nasty picture with a mean note and left it in Mr. Slinger's bag. A kind

Figure 3.1

The Decision-Making Model

Scenario: The Trio and the Big Decision

Taylor, Morgan, and Brittany have been close friends since kindergarten. They walk to school and back home together, play soccer on the school team, eat lunch together at their favorite table in the school cafeteria, and they spend a lot of time on the weekends at the mall. The teacher asks the class to welcome a new member to the class, Emily. After a couple of days, the teacher notices that Emily is eating lunch by herself. He asks the trio (Taylor, Morgan, and Brittany) to include Emily into their lunchtime group. They agree and eat lunch with her as well as include her into other trio activities. Brittany begins to resent the inclusion of Emily into their tight circle. She suggests to Taylor and Morgan that if Emily is worthy of being part of their group then she has to prove herself by participating in an initiation rite. The girls support the idea. Brittany suggests that Emily would have to secretly take a baseball cap from Jordan, the "hottest" boy in class and give it to her so she could hang the "trophy" in her bedroom. Taylor is concerned that having Emily take someone else's property would be terribly mean and unkind. She wants Emily included in the group without any initiation. Brittany reminds the trio members that they have been together for a long time and they always vote on decisions. She asks Morgan, "What are you going to?"

Problem-Solving:

1.   State Morgan's problem.

Copyright © 2002 Nancy A. Chicola and Eleanor B. English • *Creating Caring Communities with Books Kids Love*
Fulcrum Publishing • (800) 992-2908 • www.fulcrum-books.com

2. Suggest solutions to the problem.

3. For each solution, state the positive and negative consequences.

4. Weigh the consequences from Morgan's point of view.

5. State the decision and rationale.

Reflection:

Describe how the decision impacts on caring in a school situation.

note and some treats from her teacher were found in Lilly's purse and caused her to feel guilty about what she had done. A new picture and a written apology to the teacher brought Lilly a new sense of caring about others over herself.

Human Rights Article(s):

> Article 28: Right to social order assuring human rights

NCSS Standard(s):

IV. Individual Development and Identity

X. Civic Ideals and Practices

Knowledge:

- Identify the behaviors that students must engage in to learn in school.
- Describe the tasks that the teacher must accomplish so that learning can occur.
- Identify the behaviors in which Lilly engages that makes it difficult for others to learn and for Mr. Slinger to teach.
- Reflect on how Lilly overcomes her feelings of anger and guilt in order to restore harmony with her teacher and the other students.

Skills:

- Gather data about the routines that support learning in the classroom and compare that to Mr. Slinger's rules and routines.
- Interpret the kinds of behavior that support or enhance caring in the classroom.
- Evaluate personal behavior and contributions to a caring classroom.

Value(s): Respect and responsibility are crucial to creating harmony and caring in the classroom.

Activities: I = Individual   P = Partners   G = Group

A. Rules! Rules! Rules! (G)

Materials: chart paper, markers, the book

After reading the book, have children identify the rules in Mr. Slinger's classroom. List the rules on the chart paper. Next, identify the rules in your own classroom. List those rules on the chart paper. Engage students in a discussion about the similarities and differences in the rules as well as the rationale for the rules. In addition, indicate how these rules contribute to a caring classroom.

Questions to Ask:

1. Which rules are the same on both charts?
2. Which rules are different?
3. Why are there rules to follow in both classrooms? How do they show that you care for your classmates?
4. Which three rules best demonstrate caring for classmates by helping students learn? Explain.

B. To My Teacher: Letters from the Class (I, P, G)

Materials: primary lined paper, pencils, crayons

Individually, the students think about the aspects of their classroom and teacher that they enjoy and show that the teacher cares for them and that they care for the teacher. Then in pairs, the children discuss all of the things they like about their teacher and the class. They share their responses with the class while the teacher records some idea words on the board for use in their writing. The children, individually, compose letters with pictures to their teacher that include caring ideas about what they like about the teacher and class. Post the letters on the bulletin board and discuss the letters.

C. My Caring Journal (I)

Materials: small hard-covered notebook for journal writing, pencils, crayons

Based on the responses to the *Questions to Ask* (A) and the *Letters to the Teacher* (B), students record actions they take to support their caring classroom. Each entry should be dated, the action described, identify to whom the behavior was directed, and list the feelings of the recipient and personal feelings. This journal should be ongoing with sharing at the end of each week so that children's caring behaviors are reinforced.

The Story of Ruby Bridges

The Connection: *The Story of Ruby Bridges* by Robert Coles, 1995
Genre: Biography, Picture Book
Level: Bridge
Reader: Student
The Book: In 1960, Ruby Bridges broke the racial divide in the New Orleans schools by being the first black child to enter first grade at a previously all-white elementary school. Everyday for months, she was escorted by federal marshals past an angry white mob shouting obscenities.

As the parents of white children kept them at home, Ruby worked alone in the classroom with her teacher to learn how to read and write. Throughout this ordeal, she remained calm and courageous with the help of her faith and family support. Eventually, white children began to return, and Ruby completed her education at that newly integrated elementary school.

Human Rights Article(s):

Article 1: Right to equality

Article 2: Freedom from discrimination

Article 3: Right to life, liberty, and personal security

Article 7: Right to equality before the law

Article 26: Right to education

NCSS Standard(s):

I. Culture

II. Time, Continuity, and Change

IV. Individual Development and Identity

V. Individuals, Groups, and Institutions

X. Civic Ideals and Practices

Knowledge:

* Define segregation as it relates to schools.
* Describe the unfairness of segregation in the schools in New Orleans in 1960.
* Explain the feelings of fear and hatred that surround the desegregation of schools in New Orleans.
* Detail the role that the federal government played in Ruby's days at Frantz Elementary School.
* Describe the behavior and feelings that Ruby demonstrated during her daily ordeal of passing by the angry crowd at the school entrance and as the only black child in the school.
* Determine ways in which the schools and discriminatory attitudes have changed since Ruby's ordeal in 1960.

Skills:

* Search for web-based sources of information about Ruby Bridges and about past practices of school segregation.
* Summarize the feelings that Ruby had during the ordeal.
* Using the I-BE-IT© Model, empathize with Ruby's feelings.
* Evaluate any unfair situation that could lead to discrimination in your school.
* Create laws for your school to prevent discrimination.

Value(s): Schools in a democratic society should reflect and provide the highest degree of justice for all. Students should never feel a sense of unfairness through discrimination in any school.

Activities: I = Individual   P = Partners   G = Group

A. The Search for Justice (P)

Materials: computer(s) with Internet capability and sound card, printer, paper, pencils

In partner teams, search web-based sources for information about Ruby Bridges today and in the past. Also find information about school segregation/desegregation. Print data from websites. In their search, students will discover audio as well as video information. In this situation, handwritten notes could be taken on pertinent data. Analyze both sets of data for emotions and behaviors demonstrated by supporters and opponents of school desegregation. In team discussions, respond to the following questions.

Questions to Ask:
1. How would you define school segregation?
2. Why was school segregation unfair?
3. What were the feelings and actions of the segregationists in New Orleans?
4. Why would Ruby Bridges be considered a hero?

B. I Feel What Ruby Feels (G)

Materials: the book (use pages from Ruby's first day at school to the day when she stopped and prayed before the angry crowd), paper, pencils, I-BE-IT Model (Appendix C)

The teacher uses the initial phase of the I-BE-IT Model (Appendix C) to lead students through a personal happy or sad experience from the past. In the Pre-Reflection phase, *Identification*, the teacher and students discuss the characteristics of Ruby that could be matched to characteristics of students in the class (e.g., age, family, location, school, recreation). In the Reflection phase, the students sit back with eyes closed while the teacher takes them through the *Bracketing* component. Teacher sets the scene by describing where the action takes place and the interrelationships and attitudes of the people within the scene. With the students listening, teacher reads the selected pages from *Ruby Bridges*. During *Empathy*, the teacher says, "Now, you are Ruby Bridges, put yourself in her place and look through her eyes. Experience what she experiences; feel what she feels." Some questions to guide the empathetic experience: What do you see? How does it make you feel when you first see the mob at the school entrance? How do you feel when you realize that you are the only child attending the school? How did you feel about those people when you stopped and prayed? Have the children open their eyes, pick up their pencils and write a description of their feelings during that lived moment and share those with the class. During the Post-Reflection phase, *Insight*, ask questions about the action that Ruby took (e.g., What caring action did Ruby take? In Ruby's place would you have done the same thing? What were the consequences of her caring actions? How do you think this affected the lives of other children and adults living then and now? In *Transference*, the teacher leads a discussion that connects the feelings about being caring that were aroused and resulted from this sharing of the lived experience with an historical character to the attitudes and actions in today's world. Following are some possible guiding questions to ask. How can you follow Ruby's example by being caring in your own school? Can you think of any unfair situations in which you could feel a concern for other human beings in your school? What actions could you take to change these unfair situations?

C. There Ought to Be a Law (P)

Materials: paper, pencils, poster board, markers

Based on the empathy, genuine understandings, and transference resulting from the I-BE-IT© process, students, in partner teams, brainstorm any unfair situations that could lead to discrimination in their school. Record and evaluate each situation. Choose the most unfair situations and then create a list of laws (displayed on poster board) that could possibly prevent these situations from occurring. Chose a title for each poster. Partners present their laws to the class and explain how they could be implemented and followed at their school. Display the posters in the halls for all to read and adopt.

Harry Potter and the Sorcerer's Stone

The Connection: *Harry Potter and the Sorcerer's Stone* by J. K. Rowling, 1999

Genre: Fiction, Chapter Book

Level: Intermediate

Reader: Teacher & Student

The Book: While living a miserable life with his aunt and uncle, the Dursleys, the orphaned Harry had to endure a horrible experience at school, as well. But things were about to change, when on Harry Potter's eleventh birthday, Professors McGonagall and Dumbledore's magic resulted in his enrollment at Hogwarts School. As a proud member of Gryffindor House Harry made new friends and was involved in upholding the honor of his house against the nefarious plots of his nemesis, Malfoy. While at this boarding school for wizards, Harry played on the aerial Quidditch team, engaged in magical experiences, and learned of his destiny.

Human Rights Article(s):

    Article 3:   Right to life, liberty, personal security

    Article 5:   Freedom from torture, degrading treatment

    Article 12: Freedom from interference with privacy, family, home and correspondence

    Article 26: Right to education

NCSS Standard(s):

    I. Culture

   IV. Individual Development and Identity

    V. Individuals, Groups, and Institutions

Knowledge:

- Describe the British boarding school model.
- Identify the similarities and differences between Hogwarts School and your own school.
- Explain how the teachers and students at Hogwarts are similar to teachers and students in your school.
- Detail how the students in Gryffindor support and care for each other.

Skills:

- Using the World Wide Web and other library sources, acquire information about British boarding schools.
- Interpret the data collected by comparing the features of a British boarding school to those of Hogwarts School and to your school.
- Analyze Harry's behavior in supporting Gryffindors against Malfoy and his fellow plotters from Slytherin.
- Evaluate those actions that specifically promote caring behavior among the students at Hogwarts School.
- Participate in a group activity to construct a new model of schooling that fosters collaborate caring.

Value(s): Participants in any school setting acquire skills for a caring, ethically responsible life.

Activities: I = Individual   P = Partners   G = Group

A. Hogwarts and Other Schools (P, G)

Materials: computers with Internet capability, printer, pencils, paper, chart paper, the book, library sources, "Hogwarts and Other Schools" reproducible

Figure 3.2
Hogwarts
and Other Schools

After reading *Harry Potter and the Sorcerer's Stone*, students, in partner groups, are to collect data by doing a web-based search, library search, and reading other books about British boarding schools. Record information about the similarities of Hogwarts School to other British boarding schools. Then, compare the findings to the features of their own school. In a full-group meeting, the students and teacher, using a triple-circle Venn diagram (see reproducible) will make comparisons between all three school settings. Once the Venn is completed, respond to the following questions in a class discussion.

Questions to Ask:
1. What are some similarities between Hogwarts School and other British boarding schools?
2. Why do you think there are similarities?
3. What are some features common to all schools?
4. How do these common features contribute to caring among the members of the school community?

B. Our School/Our House (P, G)

Materials: chart paper, rectangular table, butcher paper, 8½ x 11 construction paper, rulers, protractors, pencils, markers, glue, *Universal Declaration of Human Rights*

In a full-group meeting with the teacher, students discuss ideas for a boarding school campus that would include provisions for a main classroom building, library, headmaster's house, four to six student houses, gatehouse, and athletic fields and courts. The teacher lists the ideas on chart paper so students may refer to them during the construction phase. Before making the architect's plan, students come to consensus as to the location of buildings and fields for their campus. With no more than six and no less than four members per partner group, partners sketch a campus on butcher paper and share it with the class. The class chooses one sketch as the final master plan design. On the butcher paper, students complete, with the exception of student houses, all buildings and fields in proportion to the size of the table and paper. Each partner group chooses a color of construction paper that will be the symbolic color of their house. Then using that construction paper, they create their own house by gluing it to the butcher paper master plan. Each partner group must decide on the name of their house, animal mascot, motto, and rules for caring based on the *Universal Declaration of Human Rights* (See Appendix B) that focus on individual and house rights. Label all buildings and fields including individual student houses. Using a computer and printer, students type their rules and motto in a significant font and either scan a drawing or use a clip art program to select their animal mascot and print. For each house, the rules, motto, and mascot should be placed on the appropriate color construction. In a full-class group, students create a school name, motto, and coat of arms that includes the animal mascots of all the houses and display in the center of the class master plan design. Proclaiming their new boarding school, students display their boarding school design mural outside the classroom for all students to view.

C. Caring Rights Board Game (P)

Materials: 4–6 pizza boxes, colored construction paper, scissors, glue, cardboard, 3 x 5 index cards, markers, clear contact paper, die, computer and printer

In partners, the students will design a box board game based on the boarding school model, the *Universal Declaration of Human Rights* (see Appendix B), and the house rules for caring (see B). Draw and color a replica of the boarding school model on the full interior of the clean pizza box. Include a path with stepping stones between the buildings for movement of playing pieces around the board. Leave a space at the upper right-hand corner of the board for directions. In the design, the following features should be included: a start and finish line, logical sequence of play, headmaster's house as the penalty box, four to six house team playing pieces (made of cardboard circle with animal mascot on both sides), and a minimum of forty caring rights cards. Cover the entire board with clear contact paper. Each house team creates a simulation sentence or two that reflects a situation responding to a particular human rights article and records it on a 3 x 5 card (e.g., Article 20: The right of peaceful assembly and association — All house members must join Geeks Anonymous and pay weekly dues of $1.00). Students determine the appropriate caring civic action to the simulation and record that on the other side of the 3 x 5 card. They determine the penalty (e.g., go back two spaces or houses) for inappropriate decisions and record that with the answer. Teams are responsible for making ten caring rights cards. For each game, there is a timekeeper, a headmaster, and four to five members per house team. A die is used to determine the order of play. Each team chooses a captain who completes the actions necessary for progressing around the game board. The captain for each team picks a card from the stack on the library building and hands it to the headmaster to be read. After the reading, the captain and house team have thirty seconds to decide on an appropriate caring civic action based on their caring house rules and the *Universal Declaration of Human Rights*. If the team gives the appropriate response, the team captain roles the die to determine how many spaces forward the playing piece moves. For questionable responses, the headmaster is the final judge. The first team to complete the entire circuit of play wins the game and earns the right to be called The Caring House on the boarding school campus.

CARING CORNER

Stranger in the Mirror

The Connection: *Stranger in the Mirror* by Allen Say, 1995
Genre: Picture Storybook
Level: Bridge
Reader: Student
The Book: When Sam awoke one morning and looked into the mirror he saw the face of a white-haired, wrinkled old man instead of the young schoolboy who never wanted to get old. Other than changes to his head, the doctors diagnosed nothing else to be wrong with him, so Sam could attend school. For Sam, everything was now wrong: his teacher was reluctant to let him in the schoolroom; the students teased, taunted, and made fun of him; and at recess he was the center of attention. Sam closed himself off from everyone. He was one very unhappy school-boy, for he felt no different this day than anyone before. He was still Sam. Despite his looks, Sam had one last try at being young. He rode a skateboard and did such fancy tricks that the other children were amazed. Sam's misery came to an end when he woke up and found everything back to normal.

Human Rights Article(s):
Article 2: Freedom from discrimination
Article 5: Freedom from torture, degrading treatment

NCSS Standard(s):
IV. Individual Development and Identity
V. ndividuals, Groups, and Institutions

Help! I'm Trapped in My Gym Teacher's Body

The Connection: *Help! I'm Trapped in My Gym Teacher's Body* by Todd Strasser, 1996
Genre: Chapter Book
Level: Intermediate
Reader: Student
The Book: Jake Sherman, a junk food, couch potato, was being harassed by Barry, the middle-school bully. Although he lacked brawn, Jake was able to survive by being clever. He snickered at the brawny, muscle-bound gym teacher who spent hours working out. Mr. Braun often scolded Jake about what he was doing to his body. An encounter with a science experi-ment and power explosion caused an exchange of bodies between the gym teacher and Jake. With roles reversed, the teacher became the student and the student became the teacher. The

new student, Jake, worked on building up his body and eating good foods while the teacher did just the opposite. The final victorious encounter with "the bully" and his pals caused both teacher and student to understand each other from a different perspective. After having experienced an exchange of bodies, they viewed each other with respect.

Human Rights Article(s):

Article 2:   Freedom from discrimination

Article 28: Right to social order assuring human rights

NCSS Standard(s):

IV. Individual Development and Identity

V. Individuals, Groups, and Institutions

Angel Child, Dragon Child

The Connection: *Angel Child, Dragon Child* by Michele Maria Surat, 1999

Genre: Picture Storybook

Level: Bridge

Reader: Teacher & Student

The Book: A Vietnamese girl's first experience in a new American school brought unhappiness because everything seemed different and communicating was difficult. Her only solace was a small box containing a picture of her mother, still in Vietnam, that she looked at when needed. When a classmate, Raymond, made fun of her traditional Vietnamese clothing, Ut remained an angel child by not fighting back. Hit by a snowball, flung by Raymond, caused her dragon face to appear and led to scuffling in the snow. Forced to work together so Raymond could write Ut's story eventually led to an understanding, a Vietnamese fair, and reunion with her mother.

Human Rights Article(s):

Article 2:   Freedom from discrimination

Article 26: Right to education

NCSS Standard(s):

I. Culture

IV. Individual Development and Identity

V. Individuals, Groups, and Institutions

Miss Bindergarten Stays Home

The Connection: *Miss Bindergarten Stays Home from Kindergarten* by Joseph Slate, 2000

Genre: Picture Storybook

Level: Primary

Reader: Teacher & Student

The Book: When Miss Bindergarten came down with the flu, her class rallied to support Mr. Tusky, the substitute teacher. They assumed the everyday tasks and activities such as sharing and singing songs. The class numbers dwindled as the flu bug claimed victims among the kindergarten children. Caring for their sick friends, the remaining children made get-well cards for those who were absent. At the end of the week, everyone was happy to be back together again.

Human Rights Article(s):

Article 29: Community duties essential to free and full development

NCSS Standard(s):

V. Individuals, Groups, and Institutions

X. Civic Ideals and Practices

Philipok

The Connection: *Philipok* by Leo Tolstoy, retold by Ann Keay, 2000

Genre: Picture Storybook

Level: Primary

Reader: Teacher & Student

The Book: Philipok lived in a Russian village. He wanted to go to school like his older brother Peter but could not because he was too young. One day, when his grandmother was sleeping, Philipok slipped out of the house to walk to school. Once in school, his interest in schoolwork and his skill in reading impressed the teacher. Philipok was happy because he was given permission to attend school full time.

Human Rights Article(s):

Article 26: Right to education

NCSS Standard(s):

I. Culture

II. Time, Continuity, and Change

IV. Individual Development and Identity

David Goes to School

The Connection: *David Goes to School* by David Shannon, 1999

Genre: Picture Storybook

Level: Primary

Reader: Student

The Book: Although David's life in school was governed by rules, he had a terrible time following them. His spirit and enthusiasm usually got him in trouble. He failed to sit, raise his hand, pay attention, get along with others, and remain silent when he should. The one thing David did do was write on his desk. This resulted in an after-school cleanup of all desks. When finished, David was rewarded for doing a good job.

Human Rights Article(s):

    Article 28: Right to social order assuring human rights

NCSS Standard(s):

  IV. Culture

  IV. Civic Ideals and Practices

La Mariposa

The Connection: *La Mariposa* by Francisco Jiménez, 1998

Genre: Picture Storybook

Level: Primary, Bridge

Reader: Teacher & Student

The Book: A Spanish-speaking boy's inability to speak English in first grade isolated him from his teacher and classmates. Francisco spent his classroom time daydreaming, observing the life span of a caterpillar enclosed in a jar, as well as drawing butterflies. So impressed by his drawing, the teacher entered his butterfly picture into a contest. By the end of the year, not only did the caterpillar become a butterfly and was released, but also Francisco's drawing was awarded the blue ribbon giving him a sense of accomplishment and recognition from his classmates. He learned a few English words and gave his prized picture to a new friend.

Human Rights Article(s):

    Article 2: Freedom from discrimination

    Article 26: Right to education

NCSS Standard(s):

I. Culture

IV. Individual Development and Identity

V. Individuals Groups and Institutions

Nothing's Fair in Fifth Grade

The Connection: *Nothing's Fair in Fifth Grade* by Barthe DeClements, 1990

Genre: Realistic Fiction, Chapter Book

Level: Intermediate

Reader: Student

The Book: Jenny thought life in fifth grade was truly unfair when the teacher placed Elsie, the very fat new student, in the seat next to her. Not only was Elsie a morose, silent girl who stole classmates' lunch money, but she also had been expelled for the same reason from her former school. When she was charged unjustly for stealing from the teacher, Jenny learned that life was unfair to Elsie. Ignored by her father, unwanted by her mother who favored her younger sister, and taunted by classmates for being fat, the lonely and sad girl found solace in food. Jenny became a caring, steadfast friend who helped Elsie, now a serious dieter, through several trying situations. By the end of the fifth grade, life was becoming fairer for Elsie.

Human Rights Article(s):

Article 2: Freedom from discrimination

Article 7: Right to equality before the law

NCSS Standard(s):

I. Culture

IV. Individual Development and Identity

V. Individuals, Groups, and Institutions

Rachel Parker, Kindergarten Show-off

The Connection: *Rachel Parker, Kindergarten Show-off* by Ann Martin, 1993

Genre: Picture Storybook

Level: Primary

Reader: Teacher & Student

The Book: Olivia, a student in kindergarten was excited because her new neighbor, Rachel, was going to be her classmate. Instead of becoming friends, the two girls became competitors in all the school activities, from reading to riding high on the swings. Their bragging antics disrupted the class. The teacher required them to share tasks. The girls began to realize that caring through cooperation was best for them and entire class.

Human Rights Article(s):

Article 26: Right to education

Article 29: Community duties essential to free and full development

NCSS Standard(s):

IV. Individual Development and Identity

V. Individuals, Groups, and Institutions

Horrible Harry in Room 2B

The Connection: *Horrible Harry in Room 2B* by Suzy Kline, 1997

Genre: Fiction, Chapter Book

Level: Bridge

Reader: Teacher & Student

The Book: Doug, a second grader, told of his precocious classmate and friend, "Horrible Harry," who liked to pull surprises like scaring a girl with a snake. Sometimes his pranks failed to shock others as he expected, instead they turned out helpful and enjoyable. Even the teacher liked one of his pranks, the stub people. While on a field trip, Harry learned that a prank could backfire because one of them left him sitting alone on the bus with a bee sting on his face. Despite his horribleness, Doug believed that one never should abandon a school friend when he's feeling sad.

Human Rights Article(s):

Article 26: Right to education

NCSS Standard(s):

IV. Individual Development and Identity

CARING COLLECTION: SCHOOL

Coles, R. (1995). *The Story of Ruby Bridges.* New York: Scholastic.

Couric, K. (2000). *The Brand New Kid.* New York: Doubleday.

DeClements, B. (1990). *Nothing's Fair in Fifth Grade.* New York: Puffin Books.

Duffey, B. (1995). *How to Be Cool in the Third Grade.* New York: Puffin Books.

Gorman, C. (1999). *Dork in Disguise.* New York: HarperCollins Publishers.

Henkes, K. (1996). *Lilly's Purple Plastic Purse.* New York: Greenwillow Books.

Jiménez, F. (1998). *La Mariposa.* Boston: Houghton Mifflin.

Kline, S. (1997). *Horrible Harry in Room 2B.* New York: Puffin Books.

Martin, A. (1993). *Rachel Parker, Kindergarten Show-off.* New York: Holiday House.

Rowling, J. K. (1999). *Harry Potter and the Sorcerer's Stone.* New York: Scholastic.

Say, A. (1995). *Stranger in the Mirror.* Boston: Houghton Mifflin.

Shannon, D. (1999). *David Goes to School.* New York: The Blue Sky Press.

Slate, J. (2000). *Miss Bindergarten Stays Home from Kindergarten.* New York: Dutton Children's Books.

Strasser, T. (1996). *Help! I'm Trapped in My Gym Teacher's Body.* New York: Scholastic.

Surat, M. (1999). *Angel Child, Dragon Child.* New York: Econo-Clad Books.

Tolstoy, L., retold by Keay, A. (2000). *Philipok.* New York: Philomel Books.

CHAPTER 4

Our Neighborhood

CARING CIRCLE

Our Neighborhood

The good neighbor looks beyond the external accidents and discerns those inner qualities that make all men human and, therefore, brothers.
—Martin Luther King, Jr.

The Concept of Neighborhood

A neighborhood includes people, places, and environments that are interconnected by everyday activities of the inhabitants. It can vary in size to include the street on which a child lives or the larger concepts of town, city, or county. The roles and responsibilities of people within the neighborhood determine the cultural, physical, and caring landscape of a place.

The Role of Caring in the Neighborhood

Becoming a caring neighbor depends on the amicable attitudes and behaviors of people living and working together. The art of being neighborly means that people show a respect and concern for others and a tolerance for those who are different. It also represents a gathering together to support those who may need help and to understand and respect the responsibilities of those individuals whose job it is to protect and provide services to residents of the neighborhood.

Taking Neighborly Action

It is not enough for people to value caring among neighbors, they must demonstrate this caring relationship. They must act on the values of respect, concern, support, and protection. Children need to contribute to a caring neighborhood through a variety of ways that include being friendly to neighbors of all ages, races, and cultures, working together to improve environmental conditions, obeying rules that protect others, and volunteering to support worthwhile community projects, to name a few.

CARING CONNECTION

My Town

The Connection: *My Town* by William Wegman, 1998

Genre: Picture Storybook

Level: Primary, Bridge

Reader: Teacher & Student

The Book: Chip is very anxious for he has a paper due in one day and has no topic. He decides to take a walk through his town talking to people for ideas. As he chats with various neighborhood helpers such as the police officer, postal worker, firefighter, doctor, mechanic, construction worker, and green grocer, he takes pictures of them as they work. That evening, remembering that a picture is worth a thousand words he suddenly gets an inspiration. Chip titles his report, "My Town, A Photo Essay." The story uses whimsical photographs of Weimaraners dressed in clothing appropriate to the various helpers.

Human Rights Article(s):

Article 23:   Right to desirable work and to join trade unions

Article 29:   Community duties essential to free and full development

NCSS Standard(s):

VII. Production, Distribution, and Consumption

Knowledge:

- Identify people who provide services in Chip's neighborhood.
- Explain the individual contributions of the workers in establishing a healthy, safe, and secure neighborhood.
- Describe how other workers support neighborhood life.

Skills:

- Determine the relationship of workers to the public benefit of the neighborhood.
- Construct questions to interview neighborhood workers about their responsibilities, job skills, and connections to the community.
- Based on information gathered from the interview, role-play the responsibilities, skills, and interrelations of neighborhood workers.

Value(s): Many individual workers provide services that contribute to the culture, health, and safety of the neighborhood.

Activities: I = Individual   P = Partners   G = Group

A. Camera Clicks (P)

Materials: Polaroid (instant film) camera or digital camera, computer disks, computer, photo quality paper and printer, push pins, classroom bulletin board space, cardstock for name labels, markers

After reading *My Town*, students take a neighborhood tour. Children click pictures of neighborhood helpers using the trade book as the guide. In the classroom, students determine similarities among the neighborhood workers. Then they will put photos together in groups according to these similarities. Students explain why they grouped the photos as they did and formulate group categories. The pictures may be grouped according to worker responsibilities (health, arts, safety, etc.) on a bulletin board. Depending on children's skills, students or teacher print identifying labels for each photo group.

Questions to Ask:
1. Who are the people who work in our neighborhood?
2. How are they like those who work in Chip's neighborhood?
3. How are their appearance, jobs, and job tools alike or different?
4. Why are these workers important?
5. How do our neighborhood workers help us?

Camera Clicks

B. Guess My Job (P)

Partners choose a particular neighborhood worker and discuss what that worker does. Create movements that demonstrate a possible situation in which the worker would be involved. Partners practice and then present their worker scenario through mime. Classmates guess the particular job and determine how it contributes to the neighborhood.

C. Photo Essay (P)

Materials: photos of neighborhood workers, scissors, "Photo Essay" reproducible, primary lined paper, pencils, and crayons, 3-hole punch, metal rings

Using selected photos, partners cut out the figure of the neighborhood worker that was mimed in *Guess My Job*. Glue the figure to the reproducible and draw and color the scene around it corresponding to the mime presented. Title the picture using the name of the neighborhood worker. On the lined writing paper, students write a brief description of how the worker helps the neighborhood. Compile the pictures and brief descriptions into a book. Three-hole punch the pages and insert metal rings. Display for all to read and view.

Tacky the Penguin

The Connection: *Tacky the Penguin* by Helen Lester, 1999

Genre: Picture Storybook

Level: Primary

Reader: Teacher & Student

The Book: Neighborhoods are made up of individuals who may be different. In the story, Tacky, unlike other pretty penguins, walked, talked, dressed, and sang differently. The penguin community was dismayed with this odd bird. One day, intruders came to hunt penguins, and Tacky's unusual behavior and singing confused them. The other penguins, copying the horrible singing, worked together with Tacky to save their icy neighborhood. Although different, Tacky was now accepted by the other penguins.

Human Rights Article(s):

Article 3: Right to life, liberty, and security of person.
Article 29: Community duties essential to free and full development.

NCSS Standard(s):

IV. Individual Development and Identity
X. Civic Ideals and Practices

Figure 4.1
Photo Essay

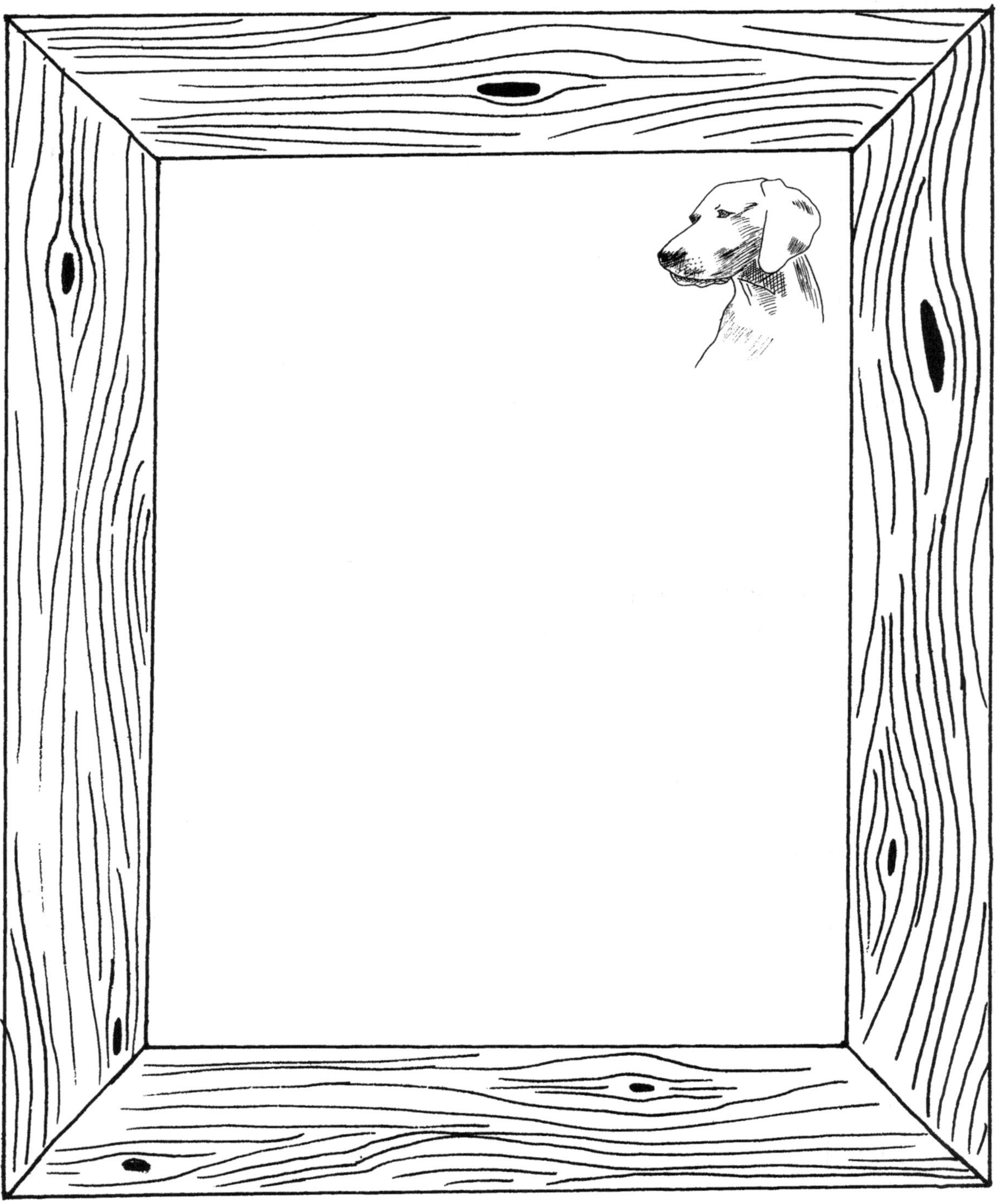

Knowledge:
- Identify the ways in which Tacky is like his neighbors and ways in which he is different from his neighbors.
- Explain how Tacky's differences brought the penguins together to save their neighborhood.
- Describe how the other penguins felt about Tacky before and after the hunters came to their neighborhood.

Skills:
- Investigate the similarities and differences of individuals in the neighborhood and compare to Tacky's community.
- Work cooperatively with a partner to develop a story that incorporates likenesses and differences among community members.
- Present the story to the class.

Value(s): All individuals, whether similar or different, can work together for a better and safer neighborhood.

Activities: I = Individual   P = Partners   G = Group

A. Melting the Cold Shoulder (G)

Materials: markers, chart paper, masking tape

To demonstrate the concepts of similarities and differences, the teacher and another adult or student should stand in front of the class. Students identify how they are alike (e.g., hair and eye color, height, clothing, etc.). Next, students will identify how they are different. Before reading the story, draw a large Venn diagram labeling one circle: *Tacky*, and the other circle: *Pretty Penguins*. The circle formed in the middle should be labeled: *Things That are the Same*. While reading the story, students listen for the characteristics that Tacky has, the characteristics of the other penguins, and those that are common to both. After reading the story, compile the information into the Venn diagram.

Questions to Ask:
1. How are Tacky and the penguins alike?
2. What are Tacky's unique qualities?
3. How did Tacky's unique qualities help save the icy neighborhood?
4. What way can you work together with others to make your neighborhood a better place?

B. The Neighborhood Tale (P)

Materials: three large chart paper sheets (lined at the bottom), markers, crayons, lined story-paper (lined at the bottom, 8½ x 11)

Place titles—Beginning, Middle, Ending—one on each large chart paper sheet. Ask children to describe what happened at the beginning of the book. Write student comments on the lined portion of the chart paper. Repeat this procedure for Middle and Ending Charts as well. Students tell the events that should be drawn in each section matching the Beginning, Middle, and Ending story events. Draw events as the children describe them.

   In pairs, children create a tale that tells how they could work together to make their neighborhood a better place. They should keep in mind the model that was demonstrated for Tacky's story. On three sheets of story paper, the students should record (in words and/or drawings) the beginning, middle, and ending for their neighborhood tale. On another sheet of story paper, students should create a title and write the names of the authors.

C. Tell the Tale (P)

Materials: laminated story sheets, colorful yarn, 3-hole punch

Punch the laminated story sheets with the 3-hole punch. Students organize the laminated pagers of their tale in a sequence and bind with yarn. The children plan and practice with partners in telling the title and the tale for presentation. Using the story sheets as visual aids the partners tell the tale to the class.

Raising Yoder's Barn

The Connection: *Raising Yoder's Barn* by Jane Yolen, 1998
Genre: Picture Storybook
Level: Intermediate
Reader: Student
The Book: Young Matthew Yoder lives with his family on a farm in an Amish community. One day during a summer storm, lightening ignited their barn and burned it to the ground despite the family's efforts to save it. The members of the Amish community banded together to help rebuild the barn that was lost. Everyone contributed in some way to the community effort. The men and boys built the barn, while the women and girls prepared and served food. Although too young to wield the hammer, Matthew carried instructions to the workers from the master builder. By dusk, the new barn was completed. The Yoders gave a prayer of thanksgiving for their good neighbors and friends who made it all possible.

Human Rights Article(s):
   Article 29: Community duties essential to free and full development.

NCSS Standard(s):
    I. Culture
    V. Individuals, Groups, and Institutions

Knowledge:
- Describe the common practices of the Amish community both in writing and orally.
- Identify the symbolism of barn raising in the Amish community.
- Compare the traditional Amish roles of males and females.

Skills:
- Work cooperatively with other to complete a project depicting the Amish community.
- Construct a model of a typical Amish farm.
- Investigate traditions and practices of the culture of the Amish community noting specifically types of barns and other farm buildings.

Value(s): Within a community, all members should be responsible for caring for those who are in need.

Activities: I = Individual   P = Partners   G = Group

A. Matthew's Mission (P)

Materials: the book, Post-It notes, crayons, colored pencils or markers, construction paper

While reading the story, create a mind map of the responsibilities that Matthew had before the fire, during the fire, and at the barn raising. Partners illustrate each of his tasks on individual Post-It notes. On a piece of construction paper, write Matthew's Mission in the center. Organize the illustrations around the title in sequential order. Draw arrows to connect the tasks. Come to consensus on those tasks that occurred before the fire, during the fire, and those that were completed at the barn raising. Refer to the completed mind map to respond to questions. Pairs share responses orally with the class.

Questions to Ask:
1. What types of tasks did the males and females do to contribute in the running of the farm?
2. How did each individual try to help during the fire?
3. What was Matthew's special mission at the barn raising?
4. How did everyone's participation contribute to building a caring community?
5. Which ideas could you borrow from the Amish community to care for those in need in your own community? How could you put those ideas into action in your neighborhood?

B. Barnstorming the Net (I)

Materials: computer, printer, paper, Internet access

Search the Internet for information, examples, and documents about Amish barns and barn raising. Select data that would facilitate groups in building models of Amish barns. Be sure to use sources that connect to other resources and reference material that would be helpful in barn construction. Each group should select a barn model that fits the Amish farm community. Record information about possible materials and strategies for barn raising. Keep all information in individual team folders.

C. Amish Barn Raising (G)

Materials: (May vary according to group preference) tongue depressors or Popsicle sticks, tooth picks, white glue, balsa wood, sand paper, poster paints, construction paper (and other materials to complete the scene), student journals

In teams of four to five students, create a plan for construction of a model of an Amish barn. Select tasks for each member of the team to complete. (Although, all members will contribute whenever possible.) Some possible jobs to assign: *Master Builder*, *Materials Manager*, and *Carpenters*. Every team member must have a job to complete. Display finished models in a central location. Students should write brief descriptions of their barns identifying the characteristics that are specific to Amish barns. Sources for information used to build the models should be included. Reflect, in journal entries, on the teamwork that was required to complete the barn raising.

The Mitten Tree

The Connection: *The Mitten Tree* by Candace Christiansen, 1997
Genre: Picture Storybook
Level: Primary
Reader: Teacher & Student
The Book: From her window, old Sarah watched the neighborhood children as they waited for the bus. On one snowy morning, she noticed a little boy without mittens. Her concern led her to knit a pair of mittens that she placed in a spruce tree by the bus stop. The boy found the mittens and wore them gladly. Sarah continued to make mittens that she hid in the trees for the children. Searching the branches for new mittens became a game for the children. Old Sarah, watching the delight on the faces of the children as they found the mittens, felt as though she had gained a new family. Much to her surprise, a basket of yarn mysteriously appeared on her front porch, one day. She spent her time making new mittens for all of the children in town.

Human Rights Article(s):
      Article 25:   Right to adequate living standard
      Article 29:   Community duties essential to free and full development

NCSS Standard(s):
   IV. Individual Development and Identity
    V. Individuals, Groups, and Institutions

Knowledge:
- Identify different people who live in the neighborhood.
- Describe how individuals in the neighborhood help others by satisfying their needs.
- Explain the symbiotic relationship between old Sarah and the children at the bus stop.

Skills:
- Collect and share data about persons in the neighborhood who are in need.
- Classify the neighbors in need by children and adults.
- Suggest possible supportive ideas to help these individuals.
- Collaboratively, decide reasonable civic action to take to support neighbors in need.

Value(s): The common good of all citizens depends on the contributions and efforts of all residents in a neighborhood.

Activities: I = Individual   P = Partners   G = Group

A. Our Neighbors (G)

Materials: chart paper, markers, "Our Neighbors Picture Strip" reproducible

After reading *The Mitten Tree*, students will identify different people who live in close proximity to them. Then, they will discuss who might need assistance in some way. On chart paper, the teacher will draw a graphic organizer in the form of a concept chart that includes a title, and responses to the questions.

Questions to Ask:
1. Who lives in Sarah's neighborhood? Who lives in our neighborhood?
2. How did Sarah discover the needs of the children in her neighborhood?
3. What kind of needs might our neighbors have?
4. How can we discover the needs of people in our neighborhood?
5. What can we do to meet the needs of our neighbors?

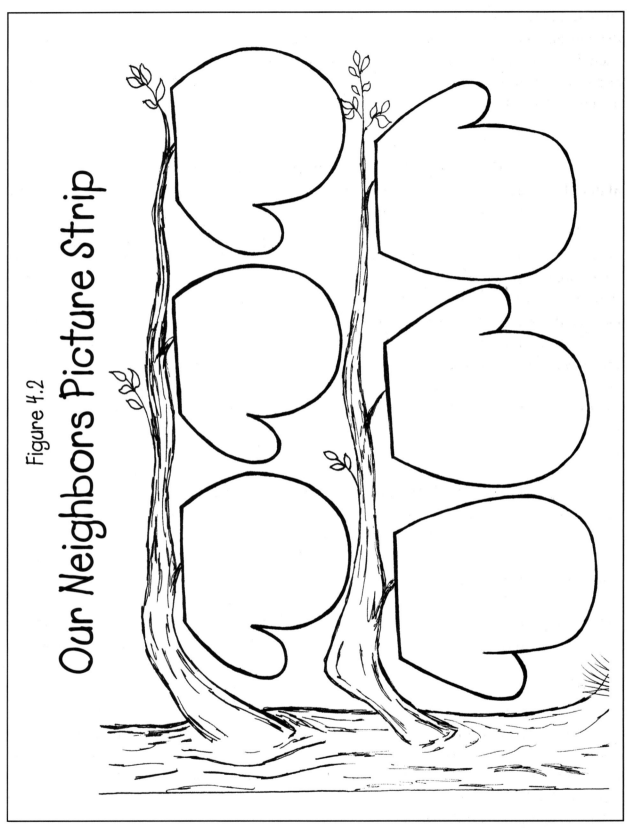

Figure 4.2

Our Neighbors Picture Strip

Once responses to questions have been recorded on the chart paper, have students determine the information to be recorded in detailed drawings of one neighbor per child. Like Sarah, they should observe persons in the neighborhood either through their window or on their way to and from school. Compile the information on a class observation picture strip. (See reproducible.) Share observations with the entire class.

B. Neighborly Action Puzzle (I, G)

Materials: chart paper, markers, 5 x 8 index cards, 3 pieces of oak tag, tape, white glue, scissors, clear contact paper

Students brainstorm all possible needs of their neighbors after viewing the picture strip. On chart paper, the teacher compiles a needs list. The children should determine three needs that are a priority, providing a rationale for their choices. Discuss as a group actions the class could take to meet their neighbors' needs. Each student draws and colors a picture of neighborly action on a 5 X 8 card. Once completed, glue the cards on the sheets of oak tag that have been taped together. Cover the picture side with the contact paper or laminate entire composite picture. Teacher cuts various shapes so that the composition takes on a jigsaw puzzle form. In small groups, children reconstruct the neighborly action composite picture puzzle.

C. Friendly Bookmark Magic (I)

Materials: card stock cut into bookmark-sized strips, crayons, markers, scissors, various stickers, one-hole punch, colorful yarn, lamination film

Using the responses to questions in A, Our Neighbors, students design a bookmark featuring their neighbors. On the reverse side, students print, To: Neighbor's name and From: First name. When completed, the teacher should laminate the bookmarks and punch one hole near the top of each laminated bookmark. Students cut a 36" piece and a 6" piece of yarn for the tassel. Cut a 12" piece for tying the tassel and connecting it to the bookmark. Fold the longest piece of yarn in half, then into quarters. Using a double knot, tie the 12" piece tightly around the middle of the folded yarn. Cut the looped yarn at both ends. To make the tassel, wrap and knot the remaining length of yarn half inch down from the tied end. To complete the project, attach the tassel by slipping one end of the 12" piece of yarn through the hole in the bookmark. Tie a knot and clip the ends. Then class discusses with teacher the various safe ways to deliver the friendly neighbor bookmark. The children should take care when delivering the bookmarks by themselves. Parents should be informed about this project.

Figure 4.3
Neighborly Bookmark

To:
Mr. Perez

From:
Shelbi

The Lilith Summer

The Connection: *The Lilith Summer* by Hadley Irwin, 1979

> **Genre:** Chapter Book
>
> **Level:** Intermediate
>
> **Reader:** Student

The Book: Earning money toward the purchase of a new bicycle during the summer vacation, Ellen, a young girl, warily agreed to be a companion to Lilith, an elderly resident in her neighborhood. In the beginning, life with Lilith was not a comfortable situation for either party. When the two discovered that they were to be companions to each other, a happy truce came about. Ellen began to get an understanding of the world and the perceptions of the elderly through Lilith's friends and activities. The most eye-awakening experience for the girl was their visit to a nursing home. Lilith was adamant about never ending her years in such a place. She explained that the residents were not learning to die, but rather unlearning how to live. At the end of the "Lilith summer" the two realized that they had reached across the years and had learned to respect and love each other.

Human Rights Article(s):

> Article 12: Freedom from interference with privacy, family, home, and correspondence.
>
> Article 17: Right to own property.

NCSS Standard(s):

> I. Culture
>
> IV. Individual Development and Identity
>
> V. Individuals Groups and Institutions

Knowledge:

- Describe the relationship between the girl and Lilith.
- Explain the changes in their relationship from initial meeting to the end of the "Lilith summer."
- Identify the feelings Lilith had about living her final years in her own way.
- Name the activities in which Lilith and her friends engaged that changed Ellen's perspective of the elderly.

Skills:

- Survey students, families, teachers, and other school personnel to determine the number of elderly relatives who are residents in senior citizen facilities, those who live with families, and those who live independently.
- In your county, investigate the percentage of elderly in each living situation: senior citizen facilities, with families, or independent.
- Compare the survey percentages to the county data and formulate conclusions about whether or not your survey data is typical of the county.
- Interview and record information about elderly living in each situation.

Value(s): Appreciate the contributions of senior citizens to the neighborhood. Be sensitive to the needs and concerns of the elderly living within the neighborhood.

Activities: I = Individual   P = Partners   G = Group

A. Ladder Links to Loving (P, G)

Materials: chart paper, markers, poster board, 2 yardsticks, poster paint, brushes, tacks, hammer

Reflecting on *The Lilith Summer*, students discuss in pairs the changes over time in the relationship between Lilith and Ellen. On chart paper, pairs sequence those incidents that demonstrate the growing bond of respect and love between the two characters. Using the concept of interpair cooperation, two pairs of students will discuss the events on the charts and add information and/or revise the order. The quads share their findings with the full class. As a group, the class comes to consensus as to the hierarchical sequence of seven (7) relevant events. Assign an event to each quad to create a rung for the ladder. For the assigned rung, each quad writes and depicts with symbols and/or pictures an appropriate representation of each episode on a 3 x 12 piece of poster board. A couple of volunteers paint the yardsticks on both sides in bright colors. Each quad places and tacks its rung in the correct hierarchical sequence, from bottom to top. Display ladder in a prominent spot for use in answering the following questions.

Questions to Ask:
1. What is the first event that demonstrates a warmer relationship between Lilith and Ellen? What is the final event?
2. How did this warmer relationship become stronger over time? What actions contributed to this stronger relationship?
3. What was the role of Lilith's friends in helping the two characters get together?
4. Which event do you feel was most important in cementing their relationship? Explain.
5. Discuss how you could improve your relationship with older neighbors. What specific actions could you take to promote this relationship?

B. Senior Survey (P, G)

Materials: computer, printer, paper, clipboard, pen/pencil, tape recorder

Students determine how they will conduct the survey and who will be included. Students could include students, teachers, and other school personnel. Before students create surveys, they must describe the focus population (seniors) of the study. This may include age parameters, gender, and former occupation/profession of the seniors. Based on an Internet search, the students list and define the variety of living and caregiving options. Once the population is determined and the questions formulated, students survey the participants concerning their elderly relatives. The questions created should help to determine how many live independently, with relatives, or in senior citizen facilities. If the elderly relative does live in a residential senior facility, students find out the type. Prior to conducting the survey, students hypothesize probable responses to the proposed questions. Interpretation and generalizations should be based on the analysis of results.

C. Senior—Student Connections (G)

Materials: journals, computers, other materials as called for by the specific activity

Students, in small groups, should chose one of the living and caregiving options (i.e., residential, social, rehabilitative, independent, etc.) and design a service project that would develop a caring connection between themselves and senior citizens. This project should have definitive goals, outcomes, timelines, and interactive activities. For example, students and seniors could become pen pals through snail (traditional) mail or e-mail or reading to seniors who are visually impaired, among others. Keep a journal of reflections relating to their experiences and activities.

The Arrow Over the Door

The Connection: *The Arrow Over the Door* by Joseph Bruchac, 1998
Genre: Historical Fiction, Chapter Book
Level: Intermediate
Reader: Student
The Book: In 1777, the British and American armies were primed for the upcoming battles of Saratoga. In the nearby village of Easton, feelings of hostility between the supporters of both armies, and fear of Indian attacks, were rampant throughout the neighborhoods. The British asked the Abenaki Tribe to join their forces. Before making this decision, Stands Straight, a young Abenaki boy, came to Easton with his uncle, Sees-the-Wind, to look into the hearts of these possible enemies. Their first encounter occurred at the Quaker Meetinghouse. Stands Straight was amazed that these people had no firearms and accepted them into their circle of friends. Sees-the-Wind broke the point off his arrow and placed the disarmed remnant over the door indicating a commitment to peace and protection.

Human Rights Article(s):
   Article 18: Freedom of belief and religion
   Article 19: Freedom of opinion and information
   Article 20: Right of peaceful assembly and association

NCSS Standard(s):
I. Culture
II. Time, Continuity, and Change
V. Individuals, Groups, and Institutions

Knowledge:
- Explain the historical context of the Easton Meeting.
- Describe the Quaker and Abenaki culture.
- Identify the feelings held by Samuel and Stands Straight before and after the encounter at the Quaker Meetinghouse.
- Compare the peaceful resolution between the Quakers and the Abenaki with present-day conflicts and possible solutions.

Skills:
- Investigate the traditions and practices of Quaker and Abenaki cultures.
- Role-play the "Easton Meeting" procedures to conceptualize the negotiation process.
- Develop policies and arguments to help resolve neighborhood conflict.
- Collaboratively negotiate consensus on the policies.

Value(s): Building a commitment to peaceful resolution of conflict is essential to a democratic society.

Activities: I = Individual   P = Partners   G = Group

A. Cultural Harmony (G)

Materials: Appropriate head gear (bonnets, tri-corner hats, and scarves with two feathers)

Reviewing Chapters 7, 8, and 9 of the book, the class will develop a role-play situation in which some will portray the leading characters (Samuel, Stands Straight, Robert Nisbet, Sees-the-Wind). The remaining students will be Abenakis, Quakers, and Frenchmen who were present at the Easton Meeting. As perceived by the students, the role-play scenario will follow the events that occurred at this historic meeting.

Questions to Ask:
1. What conflicts were occurring in each culture that led to the Easton Meeting?
2. How did Samuel view his role in the conflict? How did Stands Straight view his role?
3. What relevant factors in the cultures of the Quakers and Abenakis helped the participants in the Easton meeting come to a peaceful resolution?

4. Was their path to resolution one that could be followed in your neighborhood? Why or why not?

B. Neighborhood Conflicts (P, G)

Materials: Local newspaper

Review "local news" stories in the newspaper and identify an issue that is potentially a conflict for the people involved. Find related stories about this issue in previous news articles to make a case study (narrative sequence of events including probable causes, people involved, conflicts, and consequences, etc.) to present to the class. Based on the partner presentations of issues, students prioritize them, then choose the issue that is in most need of resolution.

C. Route to Resolution, Rules to Live By (P, G)

Materials: chart paper, markers, poster board, computer

Keeping a neighborhood issue in need of resolution in mind, partners develop rules to avoid conflict and come to consensus in the manner of the Easton Meeting. Brainstorm and record possible rules. Evaluate the possible positive and negative consequences of each rule and rank order them by effectiveness. Partners present finalized rules to the class. The class comes to consensus on the most relevant and effective rules. Place the class rules on poster board and post for all to see. Write a letter to the editor of the local newspaper about their route to resolution.

CARING CORNER

The Little House

The Connection: *The Little House* by Virginia Lee Burton, 1999
Genre: Picture Storybook
Level: Primary
Reader: Teacher
The Book: The story of a little house that could never be sold is told from its first days located in the peaceful fields of a farmlike neighborhood. Through the years, the little house was happy and content. Eventually, the results of technology and population growth not only led to roads, cars, houses, and apartment buildings that surrounded the house, but also to subway trains that rumbled beneath the house. The city expanded upward with skyscrapers that obstructed the sun's rays except at noon. The city lights blocked the moon and stars at

night. The little house was very sad. One day, the great-great-granddaughter of the builder of the house had the little house moved back to the country. The house was happy and peaceful once more.

Human Rights Article(s):

Article 12: Freedom from interference with privacy, family, home and correspondence

NCSS Standard(s):

   II. Time, Continuity, and Change
VIII. Science, Technology, and Society

My Place

The Connection: *My Place* by Nadia Wheatley, 1992
         Genre: Historical Fiction, Picture Book
          Level: Intermediate
        Reader: Student
     The Book: The author presented a unique perspective of a neighborhood in Australia. Beginning with the year 1988 and going back in time some two hundred years ago, the reader is provided with historical maps not only of abodes, buildings, businesses, waterways, and roads but also a story of the families who populated the neighborhood. The people and traditions of diverse cultures and the local and world events such as World War I and II that shaped their work and views were told through the eyes of a child for each of the twenty-one time periods.

Human Rights Article(s):

Article 3: Right to life, liberty, personal security
Article 7: Right to equality before the law
Article 25: Right to adequate living standard
Article 27: Right to participate in the cultural life of community

NCSS Standard(s):

   I. Culture
  II. Time, Continuity, and Change
 III. People, Places, and Environments
 IV. Individual Development and Identity
VII. Production, Distribution, and Consumption

Tar Beach

The Connection: *Tar Beach* by Faith Ringgold, 1991

Genre: Picture Storybook

Level: Primary

Reader: Teacher & Student

The Book: On hot summer nights, Cassie Louise Lightfoot and her family and neighbors ate, played, and slept on the rooftop (*Tar Beach*) of their apartment building. During this time, she took a magical flying tour of her neighborhood, Harlem, and all of New York City. From her bird's-eye view, she saw familiar landmarks. The George Washington Bridge was her favorite because her father helped build it. As she looked down on the Union Building, she was saddened because of discrimination her father was denied union membership and consistent employment. In her imaginary world, Cassie came to own the building and gave it to her father, righting an injustice.

Human Rights Article(s):

Article 2: Freedom from discrimination

Article 23: Right to desirable work and to join trade unions

NCSS Standard(s):

I. Culture

III. People, Places, and Environments

VII. Production, Distribution, and Consumption

The Quiltmaker's Gift

The Connection: *The Quiltmaker's Gift* by Jeff Brumbeau, 2000

Genre: Picture Storybook, Fable

Level: Intermediate

Reader: Student

The Book: A caring quiltmaker who lived in the mountains spent her life creating and giving away quilts to the poor and homeless in her community. Meanwhile, there was a king who loved receiving gifts from the people in his kingdom. He was so greedy that he never felt he had enough, yet he was unhappy. When he heard of the quiltmaker's beautiful quilts, he decided that he must have one to add to his treasure trove. He went to the mountains in search of the quiltmaker and a gift of a quilt. The quiltmaker refused the "rich" king's request. She said that if the king would give all of his treasures away, she would make a square for each donation. The king was angered and twice tried to imprison her. She still held to her original proposal. Finally, the king agreed and began to give away all of his treasures, starting small and progressing to distribute almost everything. The quiltmaker sewed a quilt for the king, but he would only take it if she would take his throne as her work chair, in return. The king was now happy from the satisfaction of making others happy through giving. The quiltmaker continued making quilts for the poor and homeless.

Human Rights Article(s):

      Article 3: Right to life, liberty, personal security

      Article 9: Freedom from arbitrary arrest and exile

     Article 29: Community duties essential to free and full development

NCSS Standard(s):

   IV. Individual Development and Identity

    V. Power, Authority, and Governance

   VI. Production, Distribution, and Consumption

Witch Hunt: It Happened in Salem Village

The Connection: *Witch Hunt: It Happened in Salem Village* by Stephen Krensky, 1989

       Genre: Historical Chapter Book

        Level: Intermediate

     Reader: Student

The Book: It was 1692 and in Salem, Massachusetts, something startling and frightening happened. Young girls were shrieking, shaking, speaking strange words, and seeing ghostly images and specters. The only explanation for this uncommon behavior was witchcraft. The ministers and magistrates demanded to know who was bewitching the girls. Fearing punishment for their actions, which had started as a secret game, the girls accused certain villagers of being in league with the devil. The girls became the star witnesses at the witch trials that ended with eleven people hanged for being convicted of witchcraft. The witch-hunt hysteria lessened when the ministers began to fear that innocent people were being condemned. The girls were never asked to explain their behavior and were never punished. In 1706, one woman confessed and begged forgiveness for her youthful actions. One guilty secret had led to the wrongful deaths of some of her innocent Salem neighbors.

Human Rights Article(s):

      Article 6: Right to recognition as a person before the law

      Article 7: Right to equality before the law

    Article 10: Right to a fair public hearing

NCSS Standard(s):

    II. Time, Continuity, and Change

     V. Individuals, Groups, and Institutions

   VI. Power, Authority, and Governance

Smoky Night

The Connection: *Smoky Night* by Eve Bunting, 1994

Genre: Picture Storybook

Level: Bridge

Reader: Student

The Book: Mama and Daniel watched the Los Angeles riots from their apartment window. People on the streets acted out their anger by looting and destroying property. Later a scared Daniel goes to bed only to be awakened by a fire. He and his mother along with neighbors flee the building for the safety of a shelter in a church hall. Daniel lost his cat, Jasmine, in the disruption. Later, a firefighter found Jasmine and a neighbor's cat and brought them to the shelter. The two cats, normally intolerant of each other, teach the neighbors a lesson of tolerance and friendship.

Human Rights Article(s):

Article 1: Right to equality

Article 28: Right to social order assuring human rights

NCSS Standard(s):

I. Culture

IV. Individual Development and Identity

V. Individuals, Groups, and Institutions

Baseball in the Barrios

The Connection: *Baseball in the Barrios* by Henry Horenstein, 1997

Genre: Nonfiction, Picture Book

Level: Intermediate

Reader: Student

The Book: Hubaldo, a fifth grader, told about baseball, *béisbal*, as it is played in the neighborhoods, the barrios, throughout Venezuela. There are organized leagues for various age levels with appropriate uniforms and equipment. Although Hubaldo plays in the Infantels league, his love of the sport finds him using all his free time to play pick-up games on a variety of surfaces with materials that could be adapted as equipment. Rolled-up socks have been used as balls while wooden planks have made useful bats. Hubaldo and other boys in the Barrio care for the game and follow their heroes who play in the Venezuelan professional leagues.

Human Rights Article(s):

Article 23: Right to rest and leisure

Article 25: Right to adequate living standard

Article 27: Right to participate in the cultural life of community

NCSS Standard(s):

    I. Culture

  IV. Individual Development and Identity

Not So Very Long Ago: Life in a Small Country Village

  The Connection: *Not So Very Long Ago: Life in a Small Country Village* by Philippe Fix, 1994

        Genre: Picture Storybook

         Level: Bridge, Intermediate

      Reader: Student

        The Book: Drawn with intricate detail, the author/illustrator has provided a glimpse of what it was like for many of our antecedents living in a small village somewhere in Europe in the late nineteenth century. The story revolved around the lives of John and Laura, the children of Elizabeth and Anton, the peddler, as they did the chores at home, went to school, and visited the neighborhood workers who provided services for the small village. The artisans such as the tailor, glassblower, weaver, and clog maker showed the children how their jobs were done. Children did not spend all of their time at work. They enjoyed the attractions and bustle of the village fair where goods were bought and bartered. Once a year the village celebrated its patron saint day with foods, games, and contests.

Human Rights Article(s):

    Article 23: Right to desirable work and to join trade unions

    Article 24: Right to rest and leisure

    Article 25: Right to an adequate living standard

NCSS Standard(s):

    I. Culture

   II. Time, Continuity, and Change

  VII. Production, Distribution, and Consumption

On My Street

  The Connection: *On My Street* by Eve Merriam, 2000

        Genre: Picture Storybook

         Level: Primary

      Reader: Teacher & Student

        The Book: Using rhyming couplets to describe each neighbor, a small boy noted the various people in his neighborhood. The neighbors, such as the grocer, jogger, momma with her twins, the dog walker, and the helpful firefighters in their truck, are presented in a no-frills, simplistic manner. The friendliness and caring of the neighbors is clearly evident.

Human Rights Article(s):

> Article 27:   Right to participate in the cultural life of community

NCSS Standard(s):

I. Culture

V. Individuals, Groups, and Institutions

Uptown

The Connection: *Uptown* by Bryan Collier, 2000

Genre: Picture Storybook

Level: Primary

Reader: Teacher & Student

The Book: A young boy described the characteristics of his neighborhood, Harlem. Using one-line sentences, the boy gave the reader an impression of what uptown was to him. This included the types of houses, foods, and entertainment, particularly jazz. A caring portrait was painted by a boy who truly loved his neighborhood.

Human Rights Article(s):

> Article 3:   Right to life, liberty, personal security

> Article 27:   Right to participate in the cultural life of community

NCSS Standard(s):

I. Culture

V. Individuals, Groups, and Institutions

Pinky and Rex and the New Neighbors

The Connection: *Pinky and Rex and the New Neighbors* by James Howe, 1997

Genre: Fiction, Chapter Book

Level: Primary, Bridge

Reader: Teacher & Student

The Book: Rex's neighbor who baked cookies for Rex and her friend Pinky was moving to the nearby Senior Residence. This made Rex sad and anxious about the unknown new neighbor who would be moving in. Rex's fears came true when Ollie, an obnoxious, self-centered braggart, came to view the house came to view the house with his mom. If he was to move in, it would be horrible. When visiting her old neighbor, Mrs. Morgan kept talking about Rex's new lovely neighbor. Ollie, a lovely neighbor, impossible! But to her surprise, Rex discovered her new neighbors were lovely. Rex hoped that Ollie would find a friend and good neighbor who would help him become less obnoxious.

Human Rights Article(s):
    Article 12:   Freedom from interference with privacy, family, home and correspondence

NCSS Standard(s):
    IV. Individual Development and Identity

CARING COLLECTION: NEIGHBORHOOD REFERENCES

Brumbeau, J. (2000). *The Quiltmaker's Gift*. Duluth, MN: Pfeifer-Hamilton Publishers.

Bruchac, J. (1998). *The Arrow Over the Door*. New York: Dial Books for Young Readers.

Bunting, E. (1994). *Smoky Night*. San Diego: Harcourt Brace.

Burton, V. L. (1999). *The Little House*. Boston: Houghton Mifflin.

Christiansen, C. (1997). *The Mitten Tree*. Golden, CO: Fulcrum Publishing.

Collier, B. (2000). *Uptown*. New York: Henry Holt.

Fix, P. (1994). *Not So Very Long Ago: Life in a Small Country Village*. New York: Dutton Children's Books.

Horenstein, H. (1997). *Baseball in the Barrios*. San Diego: Gulliver Books.

Howe, J. (1997). *Pinky and Rex and the New Neighbors*. New York: Aladdin Paperbacks.

Irwin, H. (1979). *The Lilith Summer*. New York: The Feminist Press.

Krensky, S. (1989). *Witch Hunt: It Happened in Salem Village*. New York: Random House.

Lester, H. (2001). *Tacky the Penguin*. Boston: Houghton Mifflin.

Merriam, E. (2000). *On My Street*. New York: HarperCollins.

Moss, M. (2001). *Emma's Journal*. San Diego: Harcourt Brace.

Ringgold, F. (1991). *Tar Beach*. New York: Crown Publishers.

Wegman, W. (1998). *My Town*. New York: Hyperion Books for Children.

Wheatley, N. (1992). *My Place*. Brooklyn, NY: Kane/Miller Book Publishers.

Yolen, J. (1998). *Raising Yoder's Barn*. Boston: Little, Brown.

CHAPTER 5

Our Nation

CARING CIRCLE

Our Nation

And so my fellow Americans, ask not what your country can do for you;
ask what you can do for your country.
—John F. Kennedy

The Concept of Nation

Our nation functions within the framework of a democratic society. Implicit in this setting is the fundamental commitment of citizens to the basic values and principles of American democracy including its rights and responsibilities. Children have responsibilities as young citizens to know how our representative government, established by the Constitution, supports, accepts, and practices the principles of equality of rights, opportunity, and treatment through the enactment and enforcement of laws. Core values of our pluralistic society include equality, individual freedom, and justice. Citizens should embrace these values and promote them through participation at all levels of government.

The Role of Caring in Our Nation

To promote our national ideals, children have the responsibility of becoming caring participants of our democratic society. This is an ongoing process of questioning and improving the status of individuals for the betterment of the nation. As citizens, children should realize that they have a right to hold differing opinions concerning the governmental practices that may be unjust for people. They must learn to care enough to be committed to changing these injustices through legal means. Children gain a caring competence by first becoming reflective thinkers, informed problem solvers, and rational decision makers. They should take opportunities to practice these skills through service projects at all levels.

Taking Civic Action

Taking civic action means contributing to the well-being and improvement of the nation through service and participation in various aspects of the democratic process. This is a developmental, ongoing educational process that provides children with insight into the fundamental commitment inherent in a caring society. Children should initially take an active role in their schools and then their communities with the ultimate goal of participating in individual service activities as adults. Initial service activities, such as peer and cross-age tutoring, reading partners, and beautifying the grounds, begin as school service. Community activities may include projects for the elderly and nursing home residents, collection of monies and food and clothing for the needy, as well as environmental projects. It's all part of a total scheme to make a caring connection with all the citizens of our nation.

CARING CONNECTION

The Flag We Love

The Connection: *The Flag We Love* by Pam Munoz Ryan, 1996

Genre: Nonfiction, Information Book

Level: Primary

Reader: Teacher & Student

The Book: The book expresses through verse how the flag became and remains the patriotic symbol of democracy and the freedoms and rights of citizens in the United States. The red, white, and blue, not only is flown in villages and cities in every state of the Union but also has been carried to battlefields and even to the moon. Children have pledged allegiance to this emblem of the republic each day in school as the flag is raised up the pole proudly. Although the nation has honored its flag throughout the year, citizens of all ages have celebrated and rededicated themselves to what the flag stands for with a national birthday party of parades and fireworks.

Human Rights Article(s):

Article 3: Right to life, liberty, personal security

Article 21: Right to participate in government and in free elections

NCSS Standard(s):

II. Time, Continuity, and Change

V. Individuals, Groups, and Institutions

X. Civic Ideals and Practices

Knowledge:

- Describe the U.S. flag including colors and symbols.
- Explain the rights the flag represents.
- Describe how people honor the flag.

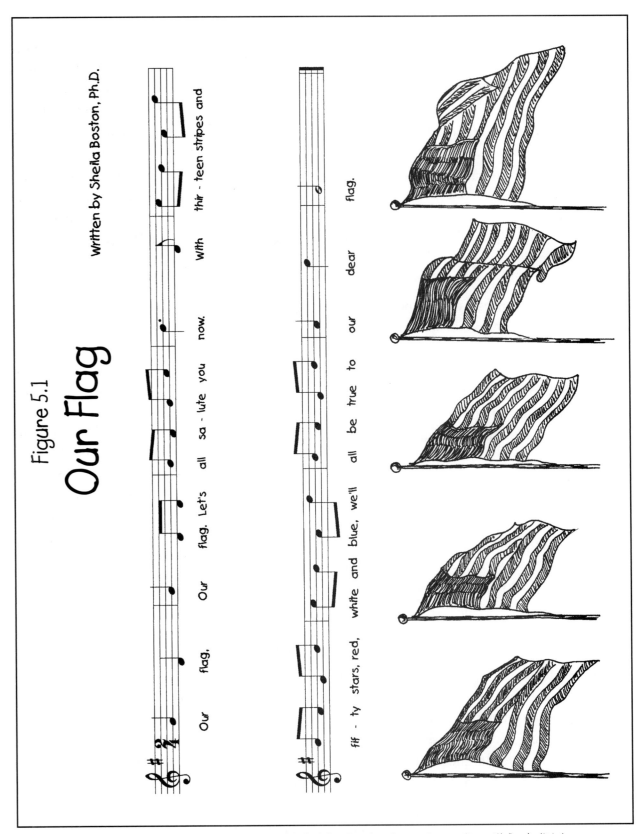

Figure 5.1
Our Flag
Written by Sheila Boston, Ph.D.

Our flag, Our flag. Let's all sa - lute you now. With thir - teen stripes and

fif - ty stars, red, white and blue, we'll all be true to our dear flag.

Skills:
- Gather pictures of U.S. flags.
- Sequence, from oldest to most recent, and compare the various versions of the U.S. flag.
- Analyze how the flag has changed over time.

Value(s): People honor and care for the national symbol, our flag.

Activities: I = Individual   P = Partners   G = Group

A. The Flag in Old and New Glory (P, G)

Materials: pictures of U.S. flags throughout history, tape, index paper, yarn

Gather pictures of flags from the book and other reference materials. Distribute copies to students in partner groups. Based on the number of stars (states) in each flag representation, partners put their pictures in sequential order from the least to the most. The teacher uses index stock and yarn to connect each card to make a chain organizer for students to display the flags in sequential order. Once the organizer has been placed in a prominent place in the room, students meet in full group to post their flags on the organizer and compare the various versions. After reading the book and sequencing the flags, discuss the following.

Questions to Ask:
1. What colors are on all of the flags?
2. What do the stars and stripes represent?
3. Why do some flags have more stars than others?
4. How is today's flag different from the older flags?
5. Which flag is your favorite? Explain.

B. The Flag in Poetry (I, G)

Materials: lined story paper, crayons, markers, pencils, chart paper

In a full-group meeting, the teacher asks the children to think of words that describe the flag (colors, symbols, meaning, locations, etc.). These words are listed on the chart paper for the children to view. Individually, the students choose their favorite flag to draw and color on the lined story paper. Then they select three to five words that best represent their feelings about the chosen flag and write the words on the lined part of the paper remembering to place a comma between each pair of words. After each student shares a drawing with poem, the flags are displayed with the chain organizer.

C. The Flag in Song (G)

Materials: "Our Flag" reproducible (see page 109), scanner, computer, LCD projector, flag pictures (from B), piano, CD burner or tape recorder with tape, miniature flags

Using the piano, CD burner, or tape recorder, and reproducible music for the original song "Our Flag," produce a CD or audiotape of the music with four repeats. Teach the song to the students with musical accompaniment. Scan the students' flag pictures and using PowerPoint or other similar slide program, integrate the music and pictures in a slide presentation. Using the LCD projector display the slide show (with lights dimmed) on an expansive wall in the classroom or other area (i.e., gymnasium) while the students sing "Our Flag" and march around with miniature flags in hand. Invite other classes to participate by singing along.

Our Flag

A Picture Book of George Washington

The Connection: *A Picture Book of George Washington* by David A. Adler, 1990

Genre: Picture Storybook

Level: Primary

Reader: Teacher & Student

The Book: The story related the life of George Washington, the father of our country. With simple, yet effective illustrations appropriate for younger students, his life is followed from his school days, his work as a surveyor, and his initial adventures as a military officer in the French and Indian War. When his duty as commander and chief of the victorious Continental Army was ended, Washington was elected for two terms as the first president of the newly formed nation under the Constitution. Washington spent his remaining days in peaceful retirement at Mt. Vernon as the honored elder statesman of the nation.

Human Rights Article(s):

Article 3: Right to life, liberty, personal security

Article 21: Right to participate in government and in free elections

Article 24: Right to rest and leisure

NCSS Standard(s):

II. Time, Continuity, and Change

VI. Power, Authority, and Governance

Knowledge:

- Describe George Washington's years growing up.
- Identify some of the important roles that George Washington played in the formation of our country.
- Explain the phrase "George Washington is the father of our country."

Skills:

- Classify the information from the book into a story map.
- Analyze the roles that George Washington played.
- Evaluate the reasons people loved George Washington and present the information in a word wall format.

Value(s): Good leaders are remembered in the hearts and minds of everyone.

Activities: I = Individual   P = Partners   G = Group

A. Washington's Story Map (G)

Materials: chart paper, markers, the book

Prior to reading the book to the students, the teacher determines the main features of the story to guide students in making a story map. Make a chart with the title of the story in the center and draw three spokes extending from the center. When introducing the book the teacher directs the students to think about George Washington as a child, as a soldier, and as the president while listening to the story (Directed Teaching Listening Activity [DLTA]). As a reminder, post a titled picture for each listening topic on the chart positioned at the end of each spoke before beginning the reading. Once the story has been read, the students share information about the features for which they were listening while the teacher records their responses on lines next to each listening picture. Once the story map is completed, conduct a discussion based on the questions that follow.

Questions to Ask:
1. What jobs did George do when he was growing up?
2. What good and bad things happened to George as a soldier?
3. What good things did Washington do as president of the United States?
4. Why is George Washington called the Father of Our Country?

B. George's Jobs (P)

Materials: markers, crayons, scissors, tape, white glue, yarn, construction paper, material remnants, paper bags

In partners, students choose one job that George Washington held. They decide what George would wear and what he would look like while engaging in that role. Using a variety of materials the partners create a paper bag puppet that represents the chosen job. Both sides of the paper bag must be decorated. Arms and legs are added to complement the puppet. Partners practice dialog that George would say while carrying out this job. For the class presentation, one partner will be the narrator who introduces George in this particular role. Using the puppet, the other partner speaks and acts out the role. After each puppet presentation, the teacher asks the audience to name one thing they really liked about George in that role.

C. Washington's Word Wall (G, I)

Materials: lined 3 x 5 cards, markers, primary lined paper, pencils

In a full-group setting, the teacher asks students to explain why so many people cared about George Washington. Then students are asked to think of and share words that describe him and his endearing qualities as the teacher writes them on the index cards. The words may be posted under the title, *Washington's Word Wall*. Using the words to aid in writing and spelling, the children write sentences that describe why George Washington was called the Father of Our Country. Once stories have been shared and posted, students should determine the quality that best demonstrated Washington's caring for his country.

Baseball Saved Us

The Connection: *Baseball Saved Us* by Ken Mochizuki, 1993
Genre: Picture Storybook
Level: Bridge
Reader: Student
The Book: With America at war with Japan, suspicion of the Japanese Americans living on the West Coast was rampant and led to their unjust incarceration at barbed-wired, soldier-guarded camps. Life for a boy at the desolate camp was very different, uncomfortable, and boring. This changed when the adults built a makeshift baseball field so that the boys could play. Although not terribly skilled, the boy took his frustration about his situation out on the ball and hit a homerun that won the game. After returning to his home, the taunts about his ancestry continued. The boy discovered that baseball could save him once again.

Human Rights Article(s):

Article 2: Freedom from discrimination

Article 3: Right to life, liberty, personal security

Article 7: Right to equality before the law

Article 9: Freedom from arbitrary arrest, exile

NCSS Standard(s):

II. Time, Continuity, and Change

IV. Individual Development and Identity

V. Individuals, Groups, and Institutions

VI. Power, Authority, and Governance

Knowledge:

- Detail the situation that led to the internment of Japanese Americans during World War II.
- Describe the feelings that the people, especially the young boys, had about their camp home.
- Explain how the sport of baseball had the power to help many Japanese Americans cope with their situation during internment and postwar life.
- Relate the discrimination that the boy experienced on returning home after the war.

Skills:
- Acquire information from the book and electronic sources about the causes and results of the internment of Japanese Americans.
- Gather data about baseball from personal experience and other references focusing on the structure, rules, and benefits of play.
- Classify the information and data into such categories as Causes, Feelings, Camp Life, and Baseball Relief.
- Interpret the role of baseball in the national culture.
- Evaluate the power of baseball to improve life's situation.

Value(s): As citizens of our nation, we have a responsibility to protect the rights of all people.

Activities: I = Individual   P = Partners   G = Group

A. Card Collection (P, G)

Materials: 3 x 5 cards, crayons, markers, pencils, computer, Internet connection

Having read the book and searched other sources for information about the internment of Japanese Americans during World War II and the sport of baseball, students in partner groups compile the information into baseball-style cards. Each partner group chooses a category (Causes, Feelings, Camp Life, Baseball Relief) to document and illustrate on cards. One side of a card should provide data in a list format about the category, and the other side should depict some aspect of the information. Partners share their card with the class, and the teacher posts them for reference to the discussion based on the questions that follow.

Questions to Ask:
1. Why were Japanese Americans interned during World War II?
2. How did the Japanese Americans live in the internment camps?
3. What feelings did the boy experience?
4. How did baseball help the boy and others in the camp?
5. What happened to the boy after he returned home?
6. Why was this treatment of Japanese Americans unfair?

B. Ball Cap Feelings (I, G)

Materials: baseball cap, 3 x 3 index cards, pencils, chart paper, markers

In full-group setting, the teacher conducts a discussion about the bad feelings that the boy experienced and how these were turned into good feelings because of the benefits of playing baseball. Students are directed to think about a personal experience that produced bad feelings. Individually, on the 3 x 3 cards, students write descriptive words that portray their bad feelings related to a specific experience. On the reverse side of the card, students are directed to record the good feelings they should have in this particular experience. The teacher draws three columns on the chart paper labeling them with Bad Feelings, Baseball Benefits, and Good Feelings. In the full-group, the students share their situations and feelings and place the bad feelings cards into the cap. Students discuss how the structure, rules, and participation in play may benefit the individual while the teacher writes and numbers those ideas under the column labeled Baseball Benefits. Next, each student picks a card out of the cap and reads the descriptive feelings words and then determines which benefits, by number, from the chart apply to help turn the bad feelings to good feelings. List the numbers of the associated benefits of baseball on the card. After students print bad feelings and good feelings in the appropriate columns on the chart, the teacher

Ball Cap Feelings

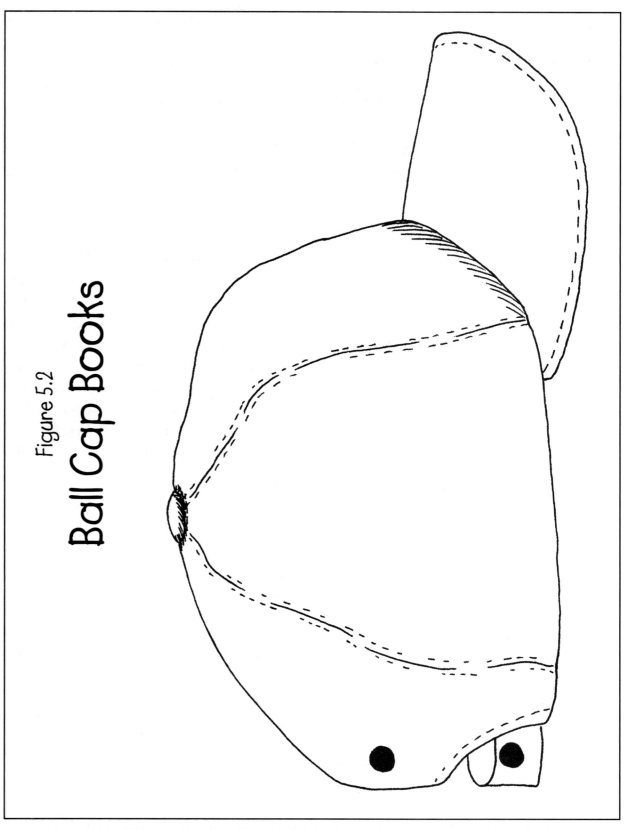

Figure 5.2
Ball Cap Books

makes a tally next to each identified benefit that corresponds to the students' choices. Students should discuss the benefits that the boy got from baseball, our national pastime. Compare those benefits to the ones students in the class identified most often to find parallels in culture and feelings.

C. Ball Cap Books (I, P)

Materials: "Ball Cap Books" reproducible (see page 117), construction paper, lined construction paper, crayons, color markers, pencils, scissors, plastic binding combs

Using the Power of Baseball as a theme, students, in partner groups, construct stories that focus on a plot where the benefits of baseball help to change a situation (e.g., segregation, discrimination, violence, etc.) with national implications applicable to a smaller context. The major characters should be people to whom the students can relate. Using the writing process to write, edit, and finalize the book, students compile a logical, interesting story that has significance for learning to care for our nation. The construction paper, both lined and unlined, should be cut in the shape of a baseball cap using the pattern provided by the teacher. The final copy is written on the lined paper. The title, authors, and illustrators should be printed on the baseball cap cover. Laminate the front and back covers once they have been completed. Insert the text (lined pages) so that the caps align, then bind the books with plastic binding combs. Display the books in a corner designated as the Baseball Cap Hall of Fame.

Nettie's Trip South

The Connection: *Nettie's Trip South* by Ronald Himler, 1995
Genre: Picture Storybook
Level: Intermediate
Reader: Student
The Book: Viewed through the eyes of ten-year old Nettie during a visit to the South, the reader can feel the girl's abhorrence of the life of Negro slaves prior to the Civil War. In letters to her friend Addie, she wrote about their appalling conditions. She related that if Addie and she were Negroes that the two girls would have no last name, would not be allowed to learn to read, would live like animals, and could be sold and separated from their families. This injustice to human beings not only made her physically sick, but also gave her nightmares.

Human Rights Article(s):

> Article 1: Right to equality
>
> Article 2: Freedom from discrimination
>
> Article 3: Right to life, liberty, personal security
>
> Article 4: Freedom from slavery
>
> Article 7: Right to equality before the law

NCSS Standard(s):

> I. Culture
>
> II. Time, Continuity, and Change
>
> V. Individuals, Groups, and Institutions
>
> VI. Power, Authority, and Governance
>
> VII. Production, Distribution, and Consumption

Knowledge:

- Describe life in the antebellum South for slaves.
- Explain the role of government in supporting slavery during this time.
- Identify the reasons why slaves were important to the South from an economic perspective.
- Compare the role/status of African Americans in society from Nettie's time to the present time.
- Describe the catalysts that brought about enforcement of equal rights over time.

Skills:

- Using the book and web-based sources, gather information about life in the antebellum South from personal, economic, and governmental perspectives.
- Gather information from a variety of printed and electronic sources about the civil rights laws and incidents that brought about enforcement of these laws.
- Analyze the treatment of slaves in Nettie's time according to intellectual, emotional, physical, and social aspects.
- Interpret and evaluate the significance of slavery and the civil rights movement to the nation.

Value(s): Every person should have an equal opportunity to participate as citizens of our nation including all rights and responsibilities inherent in the democratic process.

Activities: I = Individual   P = Partners   G = Group

A. Seeing the Story of the South (I, G)

Materials: the book, construction paper, markers, pens, pencils

Using *Nettie's Trip South* as a basis for making a mind map of the scenes of the South as a central concept, students visually depict Nettie's experiences and observations using symbols, pictures, and key words. Individuals, after reading the book, record on the construction paper their experiences with the information. Students, after reading the book, use the information to describe their feelings about the characters on construction paper. First, draw a circle in the center labeling it Nettie's Scenes of the South. Then using branches from the center that depict the categories of lifestyle of slaves, economics, and governmental actions for example, students use symbols, words, and pictures to create a visual map of the scenes. Students come together in a large group meeting to share their mind maps. Once the maps have been shared, the teacher asks the following related questions.

Questions to Ask:
1. What did Julia mean when she described the slaves as 3/5s of a person?
2. How did Nettie feel when she viewed the slaves being sold at auction?
3. What restrictions were put on slaves?
4. How did slavery affect everyone's life?
5. What do you think Lockwood's news story will be?

B. Startling Story (P)

Materials: computer, Internet connection, writing-related software, printer, scanner (optional)

Based on the data gathered from the mind maps, students in partner groups of three to four members create a story framework for Lockwood's news story. Using the Internet and other computer-based references (i.e., Encarta), students research the 1850-1860 time frame to gather further information, find any related illustrations, and verify the facts found in the book. Partner groups create an informational, integrated, and interesting news story using the verified sources. The story should be formatted in newspaper style (columns) with illustrations and/or documents appropriate to the text. Once the story has been written and edited, a headline should be created that accurately reflects the content and inspires the reader. Partner groups share their news stories with the class. Students evaluate the news stories to determine accuracy, thoroughness, and the possibility of motivating the reader to take action.

C. Steps Toward Success Magazine (P, G)

Materials: computer, Internet connection, writing-related software, printer, scanner (optional), glossy photo paper (52 lb.)

Partner groups will be compiling a magazine that reflects changes made throughout U.S. history that changed the face of the South from Nettie's time to the present. Based on a timeline from the post–Civil War to the present, students use electronic means to gather information, find any related illustrations/photos, and verify the facts about successes made toward equal rights for African Americans. As a full group, the class determines the structure, the table of contents, and stories to be found in the magazine. Each partner group is responsible for a segment of the table of contents and the related stories. Members of each partner group become involved in the research, writing, and editing of the assigned segment. Appropriate roles are assigned to each member of a partner group (i.e., editor, layout designer, research reviewers, etc.). Once stories are completed and compiled according to the table of contents, a full-group reflection in the form of an open discussion about the steps toward success should commence. Students, as a class, evaluate the status of equal rights for all citizens and determine the level of success that has been accomplished.

My Dream of Martin Luther King

The Connection: *My Dream of Martin Luther King* by Faith Ringgold, 1995

Genre: Picture Storybook

Level: Bridge

Reader: Teacher & Student

The Book: A biographical account of Martin Luther King, Jr. written within a dream format, is the focus of the book. While watching King on television, a young girl had a dream that detailed many of the injustices of segregation in the United States that influenced King's life and his work as the foremost leader in the Civil Rights Movement. She saw him leading movements in the peaceful boycott of segregation on buses and at lunch counters, for voter registration, and for equal education for children. In her dream, the young girl saw many people who wanted to trade their prejudices and hatred for hope, liberty, and love. In the end, after his assassination this trade-off has begun to become a reality.

Human Rights Article(s):

Article 1: Right to equality

Article 2: Freedom from discrimination

Article 3: Right to life, liberty, personal security

Article 20: Right of peaceful assembly and association

Article 30: Freedom from state or personal interference in the above rights

NCSS Standard(s):
    I. Culture
   II. Time, Continuity, and Change
   V. Individuals, Groups, and Institution
  VI. Power, Authority, and Governance
   X. Civic Ideals and Practices

Knowledge:
- Identify the important events that led to the Civil Rights Movement.
- Detail the injustices of segregation that were evident during King's life.
- Explain King's role in the Civil Rights Movement.
- Describe how prejudice and hatred hinder the prospects for hope, liberty, and love.

Skills:
- Gather information using computer technology about the important people and events leading to and during the Civil Rights Movement.
- Classify information according to people, events, and changes during King's short life.
- Evaluate the impact of Martin Luther King's dream on the nation.
- Create a dream vision of a better nation inclusive of King's "promised land."

Value(s): Appreciate the work of Martin Luther King, Jr. and other leaders in bringing about positive change for all Americans.

Activities   **I = Individual**   **P = Partners**   **G = Group**

A. Web of Dreams (P, G)

Materials: computer with Internet capability, Encarta, printer, the book

After reading the book, students identify the events and people as well as the injustices of segregation that are portrayed. Using a web search engine such as "Kids Only Search" and/or an electronic encyclopedia such as Encarta, students gather information about the events and people connected to the Civil Rights Movement. In partner groups, students compile their information according to subtopics (e.g., people, events, injustices, laws) and bring to the full group for discussion. The teacher fills in a predrawn web with the topic (Civil Rights Movement) and the aforementioned subtopics. Students share their information related to these subtopics while the teacher fills in the web with details.

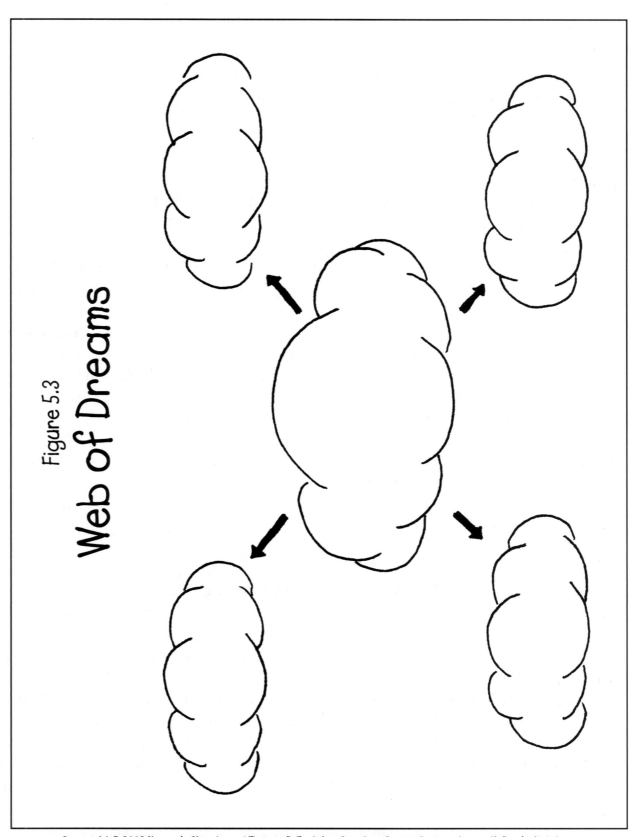

Figure 5.3
Web of Dreams

Questions to Ask:

1. What are some of the important events that led to the Civil Rights Movement?
2. How were people treated when they were segregated? Give some examples.
3. How did Martin Luther King, Jr. try to help his people gain equality?
4. How did the laws change because of the work of Martin Luther King, Jr. and other civil rights leaders.

B. Signs for Our Times (P, G)

Materials: paint-stirrer sticks, poster board, markers, heavy-duty stapler

Teacher discusses with the class some of the civil rights issues about which people today are concerned. The class may contribute ideas and/or experiences of their own. Once this is done, using the examples from the book, children, in partner groups, formulate slogans for signs that reflect the need for freedom and justice today. After partner groups get approval for the chosen slogan, they neatly print and illustrate this on the poster board and attach with a staple to the paint stirrer. The whole class determines the time and place they will hold their march for freedom and justice. In a full-group setting, the students discuss and evaluate their observations of the spectators' reactions as well as their own feelings during the march.

C. Dreams for a Better Nation (I, P)

Materials: poster board, scissors, medium-sized cardboard box, markers, crayons, tape, poster paint, paintbrushes, X-Acto knife

Using the *Dreams for a Better Nation* theme, students, in partner groups, identify and select one of the negative traits they wish to eradicate (e.g., prejudice, hatred, violence, ignorance, and fear). Each group draws pictures on story cards about what our nation would look like without this trait. These pictures may include people engaged in activities that demonstrate the reverse and positive trait (e.g., hate vs. love). Each story should be titled, "I have a dream about a nation without ..." on the first story card. To accompany the story cards, students write a short narrative that gives their vision about how engaging in positive traits can lead to a better nation. Students use the cards and narration for a class presentation in the Story-Box Theater. Based on the presentations, students determine how well their visions reflect Dr. King's "promised land."

Directions for Making the Story-Box Theater

Place the box on its bottom so that either longer side is exposed. The teacher draws a horizontal line one to two inches parallel to the top and the bottom of the box starting one inch from the side and ending one inch from the opposite side. Now draw a vertical line from the midpoint of the top horizontal line to the bottom line. Using an X-Acto knife, carefully cut on the drawn lines. Using a straight edge as a guide, fold back the flaps to create the doors of the stage. To make vertical slots on the smaller sides of the box, draw a vertical line parallel to the stage, beginning and ending one inch from the top and bottom edges of the box. Draw another parallel line two inches above the first vertical line. Connect the lines. Following these lines, cut out a slot. Repeat this procedure on the opposite side. Close and tape the top and the bottom of the box. Students paint the theater box.

Directions for Making the Story Cards
Based on the length of the slot and the width of the box, cut story cards from poster board so they can slide through the slots and extend two inches beyond the theater box on both sides. Number each card on the back in the order of presentation.

Directions for Making the Presentation
Place the cards in order in the slots, card 1 being the title. With the right hand, slide the title card out of the theater. Using the narration and illustrations, slide the rest of the cards in order through the theater slots until the story is ended.

So Far from Home:
The Diary of Mary Driscoll, an Irish Mill Girl
and
Kids on Strike!

Note to the Reader: To facilitate the young reader's conception of life for working children in middle and late nineteenth century, the combination of historical fiction and an historical information book was used. The Human Rights Articles, the NCSS Standards, and activities included pertain to both books.

The Connection: *So Far from Home: The Diary of Mary Driscoll, an Irish Mill Girl* by Barry Denenberg, 1997

Genre: Historical Fiction

Level: Intermediate

Reader: Student

The Book: The story gives a sensitive description of a young girl's journey from famine-stricken Ireland, through a perilous, unhealthy voyage, to the horrible conditions in the textile factories of Lowell, Massachusetts. The author wove an accurate scenario within the fictional life of Mary, the mill girl, living in the poor Irish section of the town. Through her diary, Mary detailed the types of work done by girls and other children and the terrors and trials that accompanied them. Mary, despite the harrowing experiences, never lost her faith that America remained a place of opportunity. The beginnings of protest by the mill girls for better working conditions and the punishment meted by the factory owners to stifle the budding union movement are also revealed to the reader.

Human Rights Article(s):

      Article 22:   Right to social security

      Article 23:   Right to desirable work and to join trade unions

      Article 24:   Right to rest and leisure

      Article 25:   Right to adequate living standard

NCSS Standard(s):

    I. Culture

   II. Time, Continuity, and Change

  IV. Individual Development and Identity

  VII. Production, Distribution, and Consumption

 VIII. Science, Technology, and Society

The Connection: *Kids on Strike!* By Susan Campbell Bartoletti, 1999

         Genre: Information Book

          Level: Intermediate

       Reader: Teacher & Student

        The Book: Based on primary sources including photographs and engravings the story detailed child labor in our nation from 1836 to the early twentieth century. Forced by poverty to work long hours in unsafe, unhealthy environments for the lowest of wages, the children banded together in an embryo union movement to change these conditions. In 1836, Harriet Hanson, an eleven-ear old, led the first strike with a turnout of nearly two thousand mill girls. She set the stage for other kid protests such as the messenger boys hoping to paralyze Wall Street and other businesses in 1897, the *newsies* in New York in 1899 confronting publisher William R. Hearst about refunding the cost of unsold newspapers, and young boys working the treacherous Pennsylvania mines and participating in coal strikes in the early 1900s. These and other kid protests led to public recognition of injustices and the passage of the federal child labor laws.

Human Rights Article(s):

      Article 22:   Right to social security

      Article 23:   Right to desirable work and to join trade unions

      Article 24:   Right to rest and leisure

      Article 25:   Right to adequate living standard

NCSS Standard(s):

    I. Culture

   II. Time, Continuity, and Change

  IV. Individual Development and Identity

  VII. Production, Distribution, and Consumption

 VIII. Science, Technology, and Society

Knowledge:
- Explain the reasons so many people emigrated from Ireland to the United States.
- Describe the conditions in factories, mines, fields, and streets for child laborers.
- Identify the reasons for these appalling conditions.
- Describe the role of children in the budding union movement.
- Explain the results of the efforts of child laborers and the union movement for succeeding generations of children.

Skills:
- Gather data through electronic means, library resources, and books.
- Classify the types of work in which children were paid as laborers.
- Analyze the information according to types of skills needed, the dangers involved, the length of the working day and the indignities suffered and the lack of redress.
- Interpret the children's role in the union movement.
- Synthesize the ideas into creative format.
- Evaluate the informational outcomes.

Value(s): Childhood is precious and thus should be treasured.

Activities: I = Individual   P = Partners   G = Group

A. Child Labor Tree (P, G)

Materials: white butcher paper, colored tape, colored index paper, lined paper, markers

The teacher papers one wall or large bulletin board with the white butcher paper. At the top center portion of the wall, place the title, *Child Labor Tree*. For levels one and two on the tree organizer, use colored index paper for title backing. Use the colored tape as branches for all levels. Divide the tree into four major sections featuring types of workers that could include mill workers, sharecroppers, coal miners, and newsies. Subdivide each major section into skills needed, dangers involved, working day, indignities, and redress. The students, in partners, research one of the types of workers and compile the information on lined paper for the *Child Labor Tree*. The information should be displayed in a tree organizer format. Use the questions that follow to help focus the discussion and prepare students for the projects.

Questions to Ask:
1. Why did Mary Driscoll leave Ireland?
2. What were the conditions for Mary Driscoll and other child laborers in the United States?
3. Why did these appalling conditions exist?

4. How did the children deal with the oppressive conditions?
5. What were the results of the efforts of children for future generations?

B. Child Labor Gallery (P)

Materials: black construction paper, white butcher paper, easel, poster board, tape, markers, paper, pencils, word processor, printer, "Child Labor Gallery" reproducible

Students, in partner groups, choose the type of workers they would like to portray in the *Child Labor Gallery*. Using the *Child Labor Tree* and other resources, the children synthesize the information to prepare for the presentation. A classroom, all-purpose room, or gymnasium is transformed into a unique picture gallery focusing on four types of child labor in nineteenth century United States. What distinguishes this gallery from all others is the use of students as part of the three-dimensional still-life pictures. On command of the gallery director, the students "come alive" to speak their prepared scenario to the audience about what the living picture represents. They engage in a question–answer dialog with the audience before returning to their "frozen-in-time" place within the picture frame. This frozen posture must be held until all frames have completed their presentations. The presentation employs the theater-in-the-round model. This complements the gallery theme in which spectators/audience either walk around with the museum curator to each picture or to turn, while sitting on the floor to visually follow the curator's tour around the gallery.

1. **The Set**

   A minimum of three pictures will be portrayed for each of the following: mill workers, miners, newsies, and sharecroppers. Each picture consists of a three-sided frame made of black construction paper attached to the wall. White butcher paper is used as the backdrop within the frame. Butcher paper, of the same width as the frame, is adhered to the base of the wall and extended four feet out onto the floor.

2. **Set Design/Costumes/Properties**

   Based on the students' research, costumes and properties should represent the historical period and be as simple as possible. The backdrop should be relevant to the topic of the scenario/vignette and should be drawn in perspective on the butcher paper. To the side of the picture frame, a caption appropriate to the vignette should be printed on poster board and displayed on an easel.

3. **Scenario**

   Each group determines the number of living pictures that will best represent their choice of the type of child laborer that will be portrayed. Students must determine the focus of each

Figure 5.4
Child Labor Gallery

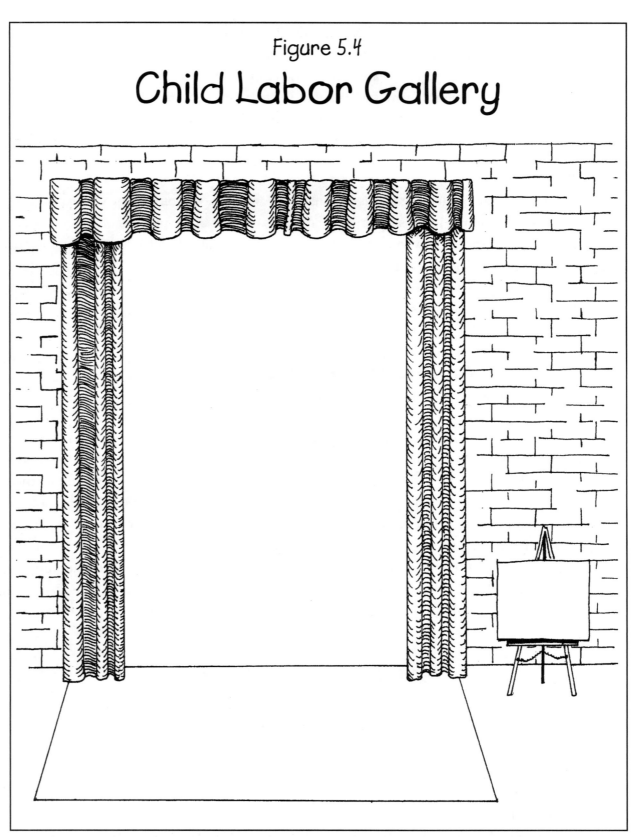

picture and record the event on the reproducible, drawing the backdrop, properties, and characters. Create the title and fill in the box area on the easel. Write in playlet (one scene with dialog) form the vignette based on the choice of child laborer. For example, concerning the newsies, the children would write about the events that occurred when the newspaper publisher expected the newsies to pay for any unsold newspapers. This vignette should be not longer than three to five minutes. Each picture should be limited to three characters.

4. **Presentation**

A curator who is elected by the class, opens the show with a welcome to the visitors, informs them of the rationale for this gallery, and conducts the tour of the pictures in the gallery. It is the curator's responsibility to write the welcome and rationale as well as a short introduction to each picture. After the curator provides the introduction, the students leave their frozen positions and present their scenario and engage in a discussion. After all pictures in the gallery have been viewed, all characters step out of their picture frames and take a collective bow.

C. Gallery Reflections (P, G)

Materials: word processor, printer, completed reproducible

Prior to the gallery presentations, feedback sheets are given to each member of the audience to complete after each group of child laborer pictures is presented. The forms should consist of the title of the child laborer followed by the questions: What two important ideas have you learned from viewing and listening during this child labor presentation? What questions do you have about the presentation? The feedback forms are collected and returned to the respective partner groups. Students in partner groups compare their expected outcomes to the comments on the feedback forms and determine whether the outcomes are met. In partner group discussion, the children talk about changes they would make for improvement of outcomes should they present the vignettes again. In a full-group setting, the children share their results and proposed changes.

CARING CORNER

Immigrants

The Connection: *Immigrants* by Martin W. Sandler, 1995
Genre: Information Book
Level: Intermediate
Reader: Student
The Book: Between the 1870s and 1920s, millions of people seeking the nation of liberty and opportunity travelled the ocean in crowded, uncomfortable conditions to America.

This historical information book, accompanied by primary source photos and drawings not only detailed the ocean journey but also followed where the immigrants settled and how they lived, worked, and where they were educated. The book concludes with a look at the new immigrants that have and are still making their way to our nation.

Human Rights Article(s):

> Article 1: Right to equality
>
> Article 3: Right to life, liberty, personal security

NCSS Standard(s):

> I. Culture
>
> II. Time, Continuity, and Change
>
> V. Individuals, Groups, and Institutions
>
> VII. Production, Distribution, and Consumption

Escaping to America: A True Story

The Connection: *Escaping to America: A True Story* by Rosalyn Schanzer, 2000

Genre: Picture Storybook

Level: Intermediate

Reader: Student

The Book: The view held of the United States by people escaping the tyranny and unrest in Eastern Europe during the early twentieth century is movingly expressed in this true story. The author related the journey of the Goodstein family from Poland to Tennessee. To trick the authorities, the family dressed as farmers riding out of town in a hay wagon leaving their possessions behind. Crowded conditions in the hold of the ship and the anxiety of Ellis Island were forgotten with the joy of being in America, the place of freedom and opportunity. For over eighty years, the family has held a reunion to celebrate the occasion.

Human Rights Article(s):

> Article 2: Freedom from discrimination
>
> Article 3: Right to life, liberty, personal security
>
> Article 9: Freedom from arbitrary arrest, exile
>
> Article 18: Freedom of belief and religion

NCSS Standard(s):

> I. Culture
>
> II. Time, Continuity, and Change
>
> VI. Power, Authority, and Governance

Dreams in the Golden Country: The Diary of Zipporah Feldman, a Jewish Immigrant Girl

The Connection: *Dreams in the Golden Country: The Diary of Zipporah Feldman, a Jewish Immigrant Girl* by Kathryn Lasky, 1998

Genre: Historical Fiction

Level: Intermediate

Reader: Student

The Book: This story of a young Jewish girl who immigrated through Ellis Island in 1903 gives the reader an insider's view of this turbulent time though her journal entries. Her life was chronicled from her entry into the United States, through her dreams and successes in acting, to her old age watching a granddaughter debut on the stage playing Mary Magdalene in *Jesus Christ Superstar.* Zippy wrote about the difficulties trying to adjust to life in America as well as the accomplishments and joys of living in this golden land. An historical note and primary source documents add historical accuracy to Zippy's journal reflections.

Human Rights Article(s):

Article 3: Right to life, liberty, personal security

Article 13: Right to free movement in and out of the country

Article 18: Freedom of belief and religion

Article 23: Right to desirable work and to join trade unions

Article 25: Right to adequate living standard

NCSS Standard(s):

II. Time, Continuity, and Change

IV. Individual Development and Identity

V. Individuals, Groups, and Institutions

VI. Power, Authority, and Governance

Emma's Journal: The Story of a Colonial Girl

The Connection: *Emma's Journal: The Story of a Colonial Girl* by Marissa Moss, 1999

Genre: Historical Fiction

Level: Intermediate

Reader: Student

The Book: A personalized view of the beginning of the American Revolution in Boston, from 1774 to 1776, was recorded by ten-year-old Emma in her journal. Sent to live with her aunt to help with domestic chores, Emma became a witness to the historic events of the conflict between the Loyalists and Patriots such as the blockade of Boston Harbor, the British occupation of Boston, and the action on Breed's Hill. The British atrocities strengthened her resolve to aid the Continental forces. Overhearing British military secrets, Emma used a special code to warn the Patriots of impending danger. She played a role in helping bring about the retreat of the British from Boston.

Human Rights Article(s):

      Article 3: Right to life, liberty, personal security

      Article 6: Right to recognition as a person before the law

      Article 19: Freedom of opinion and information

NCSS Standard(s):

    I. Culture

    II. Time, Continuity, and Change

    V. Individuals, Groups, and Institutions

    VI. Power, Authority, and Governance

    X. Civic Ideals and Practices

A. Lincoln and Me

  The Connection: *A. Lincoln and Me* by Louise Borden, 1999

        Genre: Historical Fiction

        Level: Bridge

      Reader: Student

      The Book: A young boy discovered that he shared more with Abraham Lincoln than just being born on the same date. The man who was to become the president that saved the Union and freed the slaves was once a tall, skinny, clumsy youth with big hands and feet just like the boy. Being taunted by such names as gorilla and baboon because of his looks and backwoods manners, Lincoln's caring heart ignored and forgave these personal attacks on his way to becoming a national hero. Although the boy was also called names because of his awkwardness, he recognized that his physical size and skills and good humor could make him acceptable to his peers. Just like A. Lincoln, he was a unique individual who would make the most of his future opportunities.

Human Rights Article(s):

      Article 2: Freedom from discrimination

      Article 4: Freedom from slavery

NCSS Standard(s):

    II. Time, Continuity, and Change

    IV. Individual Development and Identity

    VI. Power, Authority, and Governance

Thunder at Gettysburg

The Connection: *Thunder at Gettysburg* by Patricia Lee Gauch, 1994

Genre: Chapter Book, Historical Fiction

Level: Intermediate

Reader: Student

The Book: This story retells the true experience of fourteen-year old Tillie Pierce Alleman who, for four days, was both a spectator and a participant in the war that nearly tore our nation apart. Trapped between the Yankee and Rebel lines and cannon volleys of the battles, she observed with horror the bloodshed, suffering, and death of the soldiers on both sides who had come to hate each other. Tillie played an intimate role by assisting the nurses and doctor with the injured soldiers. When the battle was concluded and she surveyed the carnage of the conflict, Tillie came to the realization that one should never forget the consequences of war.

Human Rights Article(s):

Article 1: Right to equality

Article 3: Right to life, liberty, personal security

Article 4: Freedom from slavery

Article 28: Right to social order assuring human rights

NCSS Standard(s):

I. Culture

II. Time, Continuity, and Change

IV. Individuals, Groups, and Institutions

X. Civic Ideals and Practices

This Land Is Your Land

The Connection: *This Land Is Your Land* words and music by Woody Guthrie and paintings by Kathy Jakobsen, 1998

Genre: Picture Storybook

Level: Bridge

Reader: Teacher & Student

The Book: Kathy Jakobsen has taken the lyrical, descriptive words of legendary folksinger Woody Guthrie's song and has painted a broad landscape of our nation's natural wonders and diverse peoples at work and play. The pictures tell of the country's accomplishments (great cities, buildings, and bridges) and weaknesses (poverty and homelessness). Throughout the book, the text and illustrations make one want to sing proudly that the land belongs to everyone.

Human Rights Article(s):

> Article 3:   Right to life, liberty, personal security
>
> Article 23: Right to desirable work and to join trade unions
>
> Article 24: Right to rest and leisure
>
> Article 25: Right to adequate living standard

NCSS Standard(s):

I. Culture

II. People, Places, and Environments

Wanted—A Few Bold Riders: The Story of the Pony Express

The Connection: *Wanted—A Few Bold Riders: The Story of the Pony Express* by Darice Bailer, 1997

Genre: Historical Fiction

Level: Intermediate

Reader: Student

The Book: In this time-warp story, Kevin, a young visitor at the Pony Express exhibit at the National Postal Museum of the Smithsonian Institution, found himself as one of the relay Pony Express riders in 1861 who carried mail, newspapers, and documents to the settlements in the West. As Boston Upson, Kevin carried the news of the outbreak of the Civil War in his Mochella attached to his saddle while riding the swift ponies through the rivers, desert, and mountains in sleet, snow, and blistering sun to complete his run. Returning to the present, Kevin realized that the courageous Pony Express riders played a vital role in maintaining communication links for our nation.

Human Rights Article(s):

> Article 12: Freedom from interference with privacy, family, home, and correspondence

NCSS Standard(s):

II.   Time, Continuity, and Change

VII. Production, Distribution, and Consumption

VIII. Science, Technology, and Society

Rosa Parks: Fight for Freedom

The Connection: *Rosa Parks: Fight for Freedom* by Keith Brandt, 1993

Genre: Historical Fiction

Level: Intermediate

Reader: Student

The Book: President Lincoln may have freed the slaves, but the African Americans living in the Southern states some ninety years later were still second-class citizens due to laws such as those pertaining to bus segregation. On December 1, 1955, this situation made a dramatic turn around. Rosa Parks, believing that the law was unfair, not only refused to move to the back of the bus when threatened with arrest, but also refused to pay the fine that could have kept her out of jail. Her lawyers filed an appeal so that the higher courts could hear the case. For a year, under the direction of Dr. Martin Luther King, Jr., African Americans boycotted the buses to show solidarity for Mrs. Parks. In 1956, the Supreme Court declared bus segregation laws illegal. Due to the quiet courage of Rosa Parks, changes occurred that eventually made services available to all citizens.

Human Rights Article(s):
Article 1: Right to equality
Article 2: Freedom from discrimination
Article 7: Right to equality before the law
Article 20: Right of peaceful assembly and association

NCSS Standard(s):
II. Time, Continuity, and Change
V. Individuals, Groups, and Institutions
VI. Power, Authority, and Governance
X. Civic Ideals and Practices

The Wagon

The Connection: *The Wagon* by Tony Johnston, 1996
Genre: Historical Fiction
Level: Bridge
Reader: Student
The Book: A young boy's life as a slave is movingly told in this beautifully illustrated book. The boy hated his inability to leave his unhappy way of life. He wanted to be free to go where he pleased and not to work from dawn til dusk for the Master. His frustration led him to hack the wheels of a wagon newly built by his father and himself. For this act, he was brutally whipped. This was soon forgotten over the joyful news that Lincoln freed the slaves. Having been given the wagon and horses, the family was free to leave the plantation. For his first journey, the boy chose to travel to Washington for Lincoln's funeral.

To Be a Slave

The Connection: *To Be a Slave* by Julius Lester, 1988
Genre: Information Book
Level: Intermediate

Reader: Teacher & Student

The Book: Based on primary sources, this book provides rare data on the life of slaves in the South. First-hand accounts citing personal feelings of the indignities suffered (auctioning slaves, splitting up of families, brutal whippings) are provided. A tribute to the human spirit was their ability to hope and to survive under these conditions. The book serves as an excellent resource for projects on the personal side of slavery. Many passages are particularly appropriate for the I-BE-IT Model (Appendix C).

Human Rights Article(s):
  Article 1:   Right to equality
  Article 4:   Freedom from slavery
  Article 13:   Right to free movement in and out of the country

NCSS Standard(s):
  I.   Culture
  II.   Time, Continuity, and Change
  V.   Individuals, Groups, and Institutions
  VI.   Power, Authority, and Governance
  VII.   Production, Distribution, and Consumption

The Great Migration: The American Story

The Connection: *The Great Migration: The American Story* by Jacob Lawrence, 1993
  Genre: Information, Picture Storybook
  Level: Intermediate
  Reader: Student
  The Book: The author/illustrator used his sixty stark, yet, moving painted panels to graphically tell the story of the great migration of African Americans from the harsh, poor, segregated life in the South. This momentous population shift of people searching for a better life began during World War I when factory jobs needed to be filled in the large, Northern industrial cities. With the vision of better-paid work, improved housing, and education for the children, a great many migrants moved north. Although the jobs were there, for many, conditions in the North were not much better. Despite crowded, unhealthy housing, riots with whites fighting the loss of their jobs due to cheap labor and the disdain of more affluent, long-time Northern African Americans, the migrants overcame adversity. Uplifted in spirit by their church, the right to vote, and better schooling for the children, the migrants survived. This ongoing migration has been a significant factor in the history of African Americans and of the nation.

Human Rights Article(s):

      Article 1:   Right to equality

      Article 2:   Freedom from discrimination

      Article 3:   Right to life, liberty, personal security

      Article 7:   Right to equality before the law.

      Article 23:   Right to desirable work and to join trade unions

      Article 25:   Right to adequate living standard

NCSS Standard(s):

    I. Culture

    II. Time, Continuity, and Change

    V. Individuals, Groups, and Institutions

  VII. Production, Distribution, and Consumption

CARING COLLECTION: NATION

Adler, D. A. (1990). *A Picture Book of George Washington*. New York: Holiday House.

Bailer, D. (1997). *Wanted—a Few Bold Riders: The Story of the Pony Express*. Washington, DC: The Smithsonian.

Bartoletti, S. C. (1999). *Kids on Strike!* Boston: Houghton Mifflin.

Borden, L. W. (1999). *A. Lincoln and Me*. New York: Scholastic Press.

Brandt, K. (1993). *Rosa Parks: Fight for Freedom*. Mahwah, NJ: Troll

Denenberg, B. (1997). *So Far from Home: The Diary of Mary Driscoll, an Irish Mill Girl*. New York: Scholastic.

Gauch, P. L. (1994). *Thunder at Gettysburg*. New York: Young Yearling.

Guthrie, W. (1998*). This Land Is Your Land*. Boston: Little, Brown.

Himler, R. (1995). *Nettie's Trip South*. New York: Scholastic.

Johnston, T. (1996). *The Wagon*. New York: William Morrow.

Lasky, K. (1998). *Dreams in the Golden Country: The Diary of Zipporah Feldman, a Jewish Immigrant Girl*. New York: Scholastic.

Lawrence, J. (1993). *The Great Migration: The American Story*. New York: HarperCollins Children's Books.

Lester, J. (1988). *To Be a Slave*. New York: Scholastic.

Mochizuki, K. (1993). *Baseball Saved Us*. New York: Lee & Low Books.

Moss, M. (1999). *Emma's Journal: The Story of a Colonial Girl*. Orlando, FL: Harcourt Brace.

Ringgold, F. (1995). *My Dream of Martin Luther King*. New York: Crown Publishers.

Ryan, P. M. (1996). *The Flag We Love*. Watertown, MA: Charlesbridge Publishing.

Sandler, M. W. (1995). *Immigrants*. New York: HarperCollins Publishers.

Schanzer, R. (2000). *Escaping to America: A True Story*. New York: HarperCollins Publishers.

CHAPTER 6

Our World

CARING CIRCLE

Our World

I am a citizen, not of Athens or Greece, but of the world.
—Socrates

The Concept of World

When forming a perspective about the world, children must go beyond viewing themselves as part of their families, schools, neighborhoods, and nation and consider themselves as interconnected members of the world community. The connections among people include economic, historical, governmental, environmental, cultural, and technological aspects that contribute to a sense of one-worldness. Children, as world citizens, need to be aware of the benefits as well as the consequences of this interdependence. There is a cultural mosaic of peoples who contribute to the richness of ideas and practices throughout the world. An understanding of the cultural commonality and diversity among people enables children to accept and embrace the concept of the community of humankind.

The Role of Caring in Our World

To facilitate an understanding of the world community, children must relate their cultural practices, issues, and needs to those of people in other lands. This personal relationship elicits feelings of empathy that promote insight into the lives of others and leads to transference of caring behavior in the lives of children. An aspect of this caring for others in the world is the acceptance of responsibility to become informed about the issues, problems, and needs of people. The school plays a role to ensure that global understanding is integrated throughout the curriculum for students to comprehend the impact of global issues on their everyday lives. In a world filled with hunger, poverty, conflicts, and oppression of rights, it is important that children remain knowledgeable, vigilant, and committed to their caring role by working to provide for basic needs, protection from violence, and promotion of human rights for people everywhere.

Taking Civic Action

Using the *Universal Declaration of Human Rights*, children can make a difference in the global community by promoting these rights. Activities that help create an awareness of the abuses of human rights can contribute to changes that could make progress toward resolution of those abuses. Making worldwide connections through the use of technology, writing letters to pen pals, getting involved with groups such as Defense for Children International (DCI), and celebrating international days such as International Children's Day can highlight the abuses toward children. Other activities may include creating displays about issues, developing schoolwide awareness assemblies, establishing a human rights magazine, implementing a letter-writing campaign, and investigating and debating the consequences of the possible solutions to continuing global issues such as scarcity of resources and pollution. These caring efforts have the potential to guarantee human rights for all world citizens.

CARING CONNECTIONS

Fireflies in the Dark: The Story of Freidl Dicker-Brandeis and the Children of Terezin

The Connection: *Fireflies in the Dark: The Story of Freidl Dicker-Brandeis and the Children of Terezin* by Susan Goldman Rubin, 2000

Genre: Biography

Level: Intermediate

Reader: Teacher & Student

The Book: A brief review of Friedl Dicker-Brandeis's life prefaced a startling portrayal of her days at Terezin concentration camp from December 1942 until her death at Auschwitz in October 1944. Many of the illustrations throughout the book were created by the children of Terezin. The book is a testament to Dicker-Brandeis and her dedication to caring for others and enhancing their lives through art. She was an artist, art therapist, and teacher who spent the last two years of her life trying to ease the pain of imprisonment at Terezin for hundreds of children through the arts. She organized art workshops, contests, and plays to distract the children from the horrors perpetrated by the Nazis.

Human Rights Article(s):

Article 2: Freedom from discrimination

Article 3: Right to life, liberty, personal security

Article 5: Freedom from torture, degrading treatment

Article 12: Freedom from interference with privacy, family, home and correspondence

Article 18: Freedom of belief and religion

Article 25: Right to adequate living standard

Article 26: Right to education

NCSS Standard(s):
  I. Culture
  II. Time, Continuity, and Change
  IV. Individual Development and Identity
  V. Power, Authority, and Governance

Knowledge:
  - Define the Holocaust as it relates to World War II.
  - Describe the working and living conditions for those imprisoned in the concentration camps, both work and death camps.
  - Detail the arts in which the prisoners at Terezin were involved.
  - Explain how participation in the arts can help people.

Skills:
  - Gather information through electronic media and other library resources concerning the Holocaust and concentration camps during World War II.
  - Research the various activities included in the arts in general and specifically those at Terezin.
  - Categorize the arts into musical, performing, and visual.
  - Interpret the role the arts play in helping people cope with adversity.
  - Create and perform an arts activity that could help people cope with adversity.
  - Evaluate the impact of the arts on people to fight adversity.

Value(s): Participation in the arts can provide a sense of self-satisfaction, enjoyment, as well as an escape from the harsh realities of life.

Activities: I = Individual   P = Partners   G = Group

A. Chain to Terezin (P, G)

Materials: markers, chart paper, rope, tape, the book, computer with Internet access

In four partner groups, students select a topic to research. The topics include 1. Nazi Germany, 2. Concentration Camps, 3. Living and Working Conditions at Terezin, 4. The Arts at Terezin. Using library and Internet resources partner groups gather information about the selected topics. After recording the information, each partner group writes the important data on chart paper. In a full-group setting, students organize the charts in a sequential chain according to topics 1–4. Attach the charts, in order, to the rope that is hung horizontally across the top of the chalkboard to symbolize a chain of events. Each partner group presents their information. In a discussion address the following questions.

Questions to Ask:

1. What role did the Nazis play in the Holocaust?
2. How were the prisoners in concentration camps treated?
3. How were the conditions at Terezin similar to other concentration camps? How were they different?
4. Why did Dicker-Brandeis gather all sorts of art supplies to take with her to Terezin? What was her role at this work camp?
5. In what arts were the prisoners at Terezin engaged?
6. How were the children and other prisoners affected by participation in the arts?
7. How did you feel after reading about the arts at Terezin?

B. Escape into the Arts (P)

Materials: anything relevant to arts choices, the book, school resource persons

Teacher invites the art, music, and physical education teachers to discuss the visual, musical, and performing arts with the children. Using a triangular format, represent activities from each of the three areas of the arts mentioned. Once a thorough investigation of all possible activities that relate to the arts has been made, the students in partner groups should choose, by consensus, one activity in which they will present. Some possible presentations could be an art exhibit, vocal or instrumental concert, a dance or a drama. Students gather the materials appropriate to the chosen presentation, organize and write information for presentation, practice for the opening, and determine the space requirements. After a class or school presentation, students should evaluate whether the activities were enjoyable and beneficial from the viewpoint of both participant and spectator.

C. The Arts in a Box (G)

Materials: art supplies, plastic shoeboxes with covers, resource materials, computer with Internet access

The focus of this project is to create a box of materials that can be used by individuals to create a visual arts product that is personally meaningful, satisfying, and could be a distraction from their present situation. As a full group, the class should identify with the teacher's guidance a group or organization (e.g., children's hospital, nursing home, battered women's shelter) that could benefit from participation in the visual arts (e.g., painting, drawing, collage, and/or crafts). Once the class has selected the group or organization that they wish to help, they should determine which visual art would match the needs of that group. For the chosen visual art, the class brainstorms a list of the essential materials for participants to use for project completion. When evaluating the essential materials list, students must consider space, size, and available resources. Some resources may be purchased, donated, or provided by the school. Organize the materials into the plastic shoeboxes for distribution to the selected group or organization. Add a brief survey (3 statements) that addresses whether the materials were useful and sufficient and the activity was enjoyable and beneficial. Once the surveys have been returned, students evaluate the impact of the visual arts boxes on the selected group. Suggestions for improvement and extension of the activity should be considered and acted on.

The Day Gogo Went to Vote

The Connection: *The Day Gogo Went to Vote* by Elinor B. Sisulu, 1996
Genre: Historical Fiction, Picture Book
Level: Bridge, Intermediate
Reader: Student
The Book: South Africa was to hold its first open, free, presidential election in 1994. Thembi's Gogo, her great grandmother, was the oldest resident in the township, and she was determined to vote for the first time in this historic event. A rich man sent his personal car to take Gogo and Thembi to the polling place. Because they respected this old woman for her quest to vote, the other would-be voters in line cheered her entrance into the voting office. Gogo placed her ballot into the box proudly. Thembi and Gogo quietly celebrated the happy news of the election of their candidate, Nelson Mandela as president.

Human Rights Article(s):
   Article 21: Right to participate in government and free elections
   Article 29: Community duties essential to free and full development

NCSS Standard(s):
   I. Culture
   II. Time, Continuity, and Change
   VI. Power, Authority, and Governance
   VII. Production, Distribution, and Consumption
   X. Civic Ideals and Practices

Knowledge:
   • Define apartheid and describe the effects, especially voting rights, in South Africa for native peoples and others living there.
   • Explain Gogo's strong desire to claim her right to vote.
   • Describe the historical background of segregation and voting rights for African Americans.
   • Explain the importance of the right to vote to the essence of human rights.

Skills:

- Gather information through electronic media and other library sources about apartheid in South Africa and segregation in the United States, focusing especially on voting rights.
- Compare and contrast the voting rights during apartheid in South Africa and segregation in the United States.
- Analyze the reality of voting rights in both South Africa and the United States today.
- Present the information using a voting rights documentary via an electronic slide show.
- Evaluate the local regulations used to determine the right to vote.

Value(s): The right to vote is a universal right for all people of the world.

Activities: I = Individual   P = Partners   G = Group

A. The 5Ws of Apartheid (P, G)

Materials: chart paper, markers, computers with Internet capability

Divide the class into five working partner groups to research the facets of apartheid. Each partner group will select one of the following five areas to research: historical background, restrictions, voting rights, living and working conditions, and educational opportunity. Using the news reporters' 5Ws; who, what, where, when, and why; the students record information concerning their partner topic. On a piece of chart paper, partners label the five sections, each with one of the Ws and title the chart with the chosen area of research. Enter the important data in the appropriate section. In a full-group setting, students share their findings and discuss the following questions.

Questions to Ask:
1. Who were some of the important leaders on both sides of the apartheid issue?
2. What were the effects of apartheid?
3. Where generally and specifically was the impact of apartheid felt?
4. When and in what order did the significant events occur?
5. Why did apartheid persist for such a long time? Why did it end?

B. Voting Rights Documentary (P)

Materials: computers, slideshow software (e.g., PowerPoint), projection system, screen, scanner (optional)

The intent of this activity is for the students to prepare and present a documentary using a slideshow format comparing the voting rights history and status of apartheid in South Africa and segregation in the United States. This will require further research and use of primary source documents (photos and printed and written documents). In partner groups, the partners compile the data and select related documents to use in their documentary. Using the slide software, students prepare a documentary slideshow with speaking notes for the presentation and text and documents for the slides. Documents may be scanned or copied from relevant sites and pasted into each slide. Partners create relevant questions for the audience, one from each member, with which to close the presentation. Once the show is ready for presentation, partners should determine speaking roles for each member. Presentations and follow-up discussions will focus on voting rights. As an evaluation device, the teacher and students together develop and implement rubrics that guide valid, coherent, well-researched presentations. These rubrics will be used to guide the students and evaluate effectiveness of the voting rights documentary.

Voting Rights Documentary

C. Voting Rules and Regulations (G)

Materials: computer, word processing software with publishing capability, chart paper, markners, bookbinding materials, copy of local election regulations

In partner groups, students research the local election regulations and practice looking particularly for any areas that have the potential to increase citizen participation in elections. It could be beneficial to have the county clerk or elections commissioner participate in a class discussion of the local election practices prior to partner-group review of the written regulations. Adult support to help children translate the official documents written in "electionese" may be required. Each partner group should identify one area that may deter citizens from voting and try to rewrite the regulation to promote a higher level of participation among registered voters. A rough copy for approval should be recorded on the chart paper. Teacher approval is required before the regulation goes into writing. Each partner group writes the finalized version of the regulation on the computer and prints and saves a copy to be compiled into a new book of regulations. The book should be published in a bound format for all to review. Students may choose to write letters to the editor of the local newspaper outlining their ideas to improve election procedures and participation.

On the Wings of Eagles: An Ethiopian Boy's Story

The Connection: *On the Wings of Eagles: An Ethiopian Boy's Story* by Jeffrey Schrier, 1998

Genre: Historical Fiction

Level: Intermediate

Reader: Student

The Book: The author/illustrator's unique artwork of photographs, sketches, and paintings overlaid on an authentic robe, the shamma, provided a graphic background to this history of the Beta Israelites of Ethiopia. Told by a young immigrant to Israel, the story ranged from the conversion of Queen Sheba to Judaism to the settlement and growth of the sect in the early 1990s in the mountains of Ethiopia. Because of their strict Jewish traditions, the people were often discriminated against. When famine and civil strife caused many of them to leave their mountain home the Israelis in two secret missions airlifted 29,000 Ethiopian Jews. This ancient family of Jews found a new home in Israel.

Human Rights Article(s):

Article 2: Freedom from discrimination

Article 18: Freedom of belief and religion

Article 20: Right of peaceful assembly and association

NCSS Standard(s):
   I. Culture
  II. Time, Continuity, and Change
  V. Individuals, Groups, and Institutions
 IX. Global Connections

Knowledge:

- Describe the situation that found the Beta Israelites living in isolation in the mountains of Ethiopia.
- Explain the historical significance of persecution that has been inflicted on Jews.
- Describe the discriminatory practices perpetrated against the mountain tribe of Beta Israel.
- Detail the feelings of the Beta Israelites, as expressed by Isaiah, concerning leaving their centuries-old home and traveling to the new one.
- Identify the features of Israel that motivate Jews throughout the world to emigrate.

Skills:

- Gather information from the book and electronic sources about the discriminatory practices inflicted on Jews within the twentieth century.
- Compare the Beta Israelites situation to other twentieth century pogroms of the Jews.
- Interpret the symbolism of "the wings of eagles."
- Evaluate the results of the caring mission of Operation Moses for Isaiah and his people.

Value(s): The people of the world have a mutual, ethical responsibility to protect and support others who are persecuted.

Activities: I = Individual   P = Partners   G = Group

A. Operation Information (P, G)

Materials: poster board, colored construction paper, scissors, rulers, pencils, string, markers, computer with Internet capability, the book

In partner groups of four to five, students read the book and research information through the World Wide Web about pogroms perpetrated of the Jews during the twentieth century. Each partner group selects three to four pogroms (one representing Beta Israel Tribe) to represent on a circle chart detailing the location, perpetrators, persecuted persons, and effects of each pogrom. Students create a circle that extends to the limits of the poster board using the pencil and string. Divide the circle into three to four equal wedges to represent each pogrom. Cut the construction paper to fit the wedges using a different color for each one. Using a black marker, outline the circle and write the dates of each pogrom on the outside of the related wedge. Inside the individual construction paper wedges, write the location, perpetrators, persecuted, and effects based on the information gathered. Glue the wedges with the completed information onto the circle chart. Title the chart. Partner groups present information to the class and discuss the following questions.

Questions to Ask:
1. Why did the Beth Israelites live in isolation?
2. What happened to Isaiah's people because of discrimination?
3. How do other instances of persecution against the Jews as shown on the circle charts compare to that of the Beth Israelites?
4. What have been some of the effects of twentieth century pogroms on the lives of Jews and others throughout the world?
5. Why have persecuted Jews often immigrated to Israel?

B. Operation Feeling (I, G)

Materials: the book, paper, pencils, I-BE-IT Model (Appendix C)

The teacher uses the initial phase of the I-BE-IT Model (Appendix C) to lead students through a personal happy or sad experience from the past. In the Pre-reflection phase, *Identification*, the teacher and students discuss the characteristics of Isaiah that could be matched to characteristics of students in the class (e.g., age, family, location, interests, work). In the Reflection phase, the students sit back with eyes closed while the teacher takes them through the *Bracketing* component. Teacher sets the scene by describing where the action takes place and the interrelationships and attitudes of the people within the scene. With the students listening, teacher reads selected pages from *On the Wings of Eagles*. During *Empathy*, the teacher says, "Now you are Isaiah, put yourself in his place and look through his eyes. Experience what he experiences; feel what he feels." Some questions to guide the empathetic experience: What do you see? How does it make you feel to have the bandits attack your village and to set fire to the straw roofs. How did you feel when you discovered that there could be an escape from your mountain home? How did you feel when told that the wings of the eagle were ready to take you to your new home? When you stepped on the ramp and saw Israel for the first time, what emotions did you experience? Have the children open their eyes, pick up their pencils and write a description of their feelings during that lived moment and share those with the class. During the Post-Reflection phase, *Insight*, ask questions about the actions that Isaiah took (e.g., What actions did Isaiah take while leaving his homeland? What actions did he take when he reached Israel? What were the effects of these actions? Would you respond in the same way? How do you think Operation Moses affected the lives of others in Israel and the rest of the world? In *Transference*, the teacher leads a discussion that connects the feelings about being caring that were aroused and resulted from this sharing of the lived experience with a person who had been persecuted to the attitudes and actions in today's world. How can you follow the example of Operation Moses by being concerned and caring about those persons close to or far away from you who are being persecuted in a variety of ways. Can you think of any situations in which you could feel a concern for others being persecuted? What actions could you take to help alleviate the situation?

C. Operation Caring (P)

Materials: lined paper divided into thirds, pencils, computer with Internet access

Each partner group, divides a piece of lined paper in landscape orientation into thirds. Label the columns: 1. Problem, 2. Evidence, 3. Caring Solutions. Partners select a situation in which persecution is involved, local, state, national, or worldwide, that requires an organized plan of action to contribute to a resolution and list it under the Problem column. Some examples could include bullying, loss of voting rights, and forced child labor. Gather evidence concerning the behaviors involved in that selected situation and keep a record under the Evidence column. Partner groups brainstorm possible remedies for each of the evidence behaviors, then judge the suggestions for the most relevant and feasible resolutions, and list them in the third column, Caring Solutions. In each partner group, students make a detailed plan of action so that the caring solution can be carried out. This plan should include assignment of tasks, duration of project, form of record keeping, and a holistic evaluation of process and product. Each partner group should present the project and results to the class. Students determine ways in which they could improve the process, expand it to include others, and make a commitment to continue valid projects.

Made in Mexico

The Connection: *Made in Mexico* by Peter Laufer, 2000
Genre: Nonfiction, Picture Book
Level: Bridge
Reader: Student
The Book: The village of Paracho is located in south central Mexico. This small community is gaining worldwide fame as the home of fine guitars. These musical instruments are played by traditional mariachis as well as jazz and classical musicians. Although many villages in Mexico have remained in poverty, Paracho is a thriving community because of their one industry, guitar making. Using hand instruments, the workers slowly and carefully hone, sand, and varnish the guitars following the process that has been carried on for generations. The people of Paracho take great pride in their product and also care that this product can bring beautiful sounds to people everywhere.

Human Rights Article(s):
> Article 23: Right to desirable work and to join trade unions
>
> Article 25: Right to adequate living standard

NCSS Standard(s):
> I. Culture
>
> VII. Production, Distribution, and Consumption
>
> IX. Global Connections

Knowledge:
- Describe the Mexican village of Paracho.
- Identify the unique industry of Paracho and describe how the entire community is involved.
- Explain why people around the world are interested in buying guitars made in Paracho.
- Compare the various features, including industry, of the students' community to the Paracho community.

Skills:
- Gather information about communities (students' and Paracho).
- Classify the data according to production, distribution, and consumption.
- Analyze the success of the people of Paracho based on their community involvement.
- Evaluate the reasons for the success of the people of Paracho and apply that to successful industry in students' community.
- Create and advertise a product that meets the criteria for successful industry.

Value(s): People working together for the betterment of community contributes to a caring world.

Activities: I = Individual   P = Partners   G = Group

A. Strumming Facts (I, G)

Materials: "Strumming Facts" reproducible, pencils, note cards, the book

Using the book and other electronic media, the students find information about Paracho as well as their own community including living conditions, industry, and community involvement. Record the information on note cards for use later on the reproducible, keeping the two communities separate. Review the information on the note cards that identifies features common to both communities and record on a separate card. On the reproducible, write the unique features of each community under the respective titles and write the common features in the center circle. In full group, the children use their reproducible to answer discussion questions.

Figure 6.1
Strumming Facts

Questions to Ask:
1. What is life like in Paracho?
2. How is Paracho unique?
3. In what ways are community members involved in the industry of Paracho?
4. What is life like in your community?
5. How is your community unique?
6. In what ways are community members involved in the industry of your community?
7. In what ways are Paracho and your community alike?

B. Strumming Success (P, G)

Materials: chart paper, markers, computer with Internet connection

Students, in partner groups, search for information about the guitar industry in Paracho and one industry's product in their own community. Using the two products, they formulate three major questions for the categories of production, distribution, and consumption. Check the industry website for answers to the major questions. Display information on the chart paper in such a way to facilitate comparisons. In an oral presentation, the partner groups present the information displayed as well as the reasons for the success of guitar making in Paracho and the product chosen from their own community. In a class discussion, the students should apply the lessons learned from this inquiry.

C. Invent, Invest, Involve (P)

Materials: camcorder, VHS tape, storyboard, drawing paper, markers, crayons, and other appropriate materials for this product.

Creating the Product
Students and teacher reflect on community involvement in producing a product as in Paracho. In partner groups, students create a product that would be of interest to the consumer, improves the lives of people, and fits the needs and resources of the community. Describe and draw a mock-up of the product.

Pricing the Product
Survey products similar to the created product for comparative pricing. Set a reasonable price that would be competitive, yet profitable.

Promoting the Product

In partner groups, using a storyboard format, write an ad that will be taped as a thirty-second commercial spot. Once the storyboard and script are written, students choose the parts and practice. The teacher or responsible student can be selected as the grip to video-tape the event. To evaluate the feasibility of the product, the ads could be run on the schoolwide video system for students in other classes to view. Complete a brief survey answering four questions: 1. Are you interested in this product? 2. Do you think this product will improve the lives of people in our community? 3. Does this product meet your needs? 4. Would you buy it? Students review the responses and determine if their product would be a success.

Common Ground: The Water, Earth, and Air We Share

The Connection: *Common Ground: The Water, Earth, and Air We Share* by Molly Bang, 1997

Genre: Nonfiction, Picture Book

Level: Primary

Reader: Teacher & Student

The Book: The author used the metaphor of a long-ago village commons for sheep grazing to a problem facing the world today. The message is to reaffirm the importance of nations working together to conserve and preserve the world's global resources. Unlike the villagers of the past who could go to another area should they refuse to share the commons by limiting the number of sheep, the people of the modern world have no place to go. The air, waters, earth, forests, and fossil fuels required to meet the needs of all the people are getting to be in short supply. The author's caveat to the world is that all nations must act now or face future consequences.

Human Rights Article(s):

Article 3: Right to life, liberty, and personal security

Article 25: Right to adequate living standard

NCSS Standard(s):

III. People, Places, and Environments

V. Individuals, Groups, and Institutions

VII. Production, Distribution, and Consumption

IX. Global Connections

Knowledge:

- Identify the natural resources that are necessary for life on earth.
- Describe the sharing of the earth's resources such as fish, forests, fuels, air, and water.
- Identify the ways in which water is used in the home and everywhere else.
- Explain the reasons for the importance of conservation of water resources.
- Describe each person's role in conservation of water resources.

Skills:

- Gather information about the uses and misuses of water and other resources everywhere.
- Survey the uses of water at home.
- Summarize the uses of water in a class chart.
- Compare the results sharing the commons equally to the sharing of water resources.

Value(s): Sharing the planet's resources is beneficial for the present and future generations.

A. Water Here (I, G)

Materials: 8½ X 11 light blue index paper, "Water Drop" reproducible, primary lined paper, pencils, crayons, scissors, one-hole punch, brads, chart paper, markers

Using a large water-drop pattern (see reproducible), the children trace an outline on two pieces of blue index paper and cut them out. The teacher should cut three to five sheets of lined paper for each student using the water-drop pattern. Books (covers and pages) should be one-hole punched at the tip of the droplet and a brad threaded through the hole to hold the water journals together. Students take the journals home to survey the many uses and conservation of water around the home. They may write and/or draw their findings on the page titled Water Around the Home. Once the information has been collected, the students meet as a full class to share their findings that are recorded on the class chart by the teacher.

Questions to Ask:

1. What ways is water used around the home?
2. What do your parents do to save water around the home?
3. How can water be saved so that there will be enough to share for everyone?

Figure 6.2
Water Drop

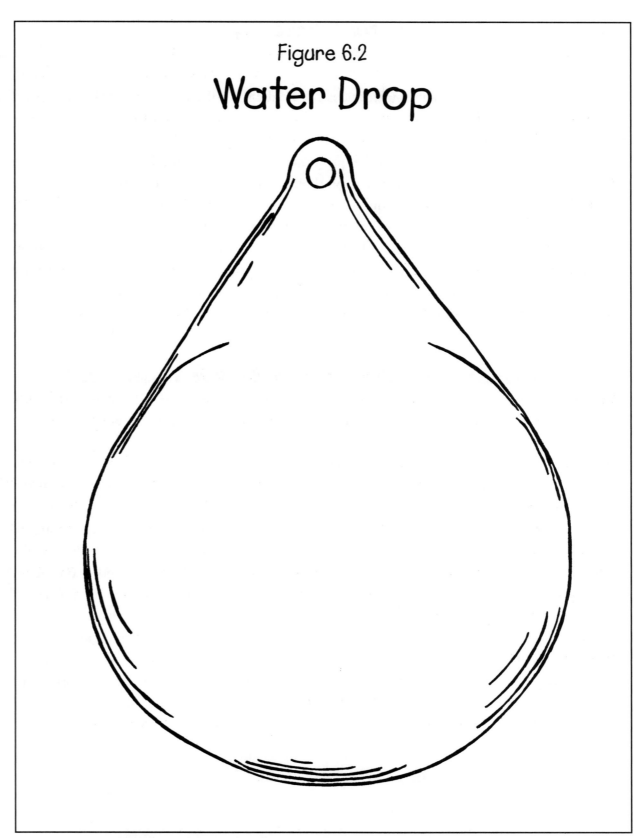

B. Water There (P, G)

Materials: water journals, pencil, chart paper, crayons

In a full-group setting, the teacher introduces the field trip to the local water treatment plant explaining its purpose for the community. Students are invited to formulate questions they may have about such areas as how water is treated, how water gets to the community, and what workers do at the treatment plant. List the questions on chart paper and have children, in each partner group, choose two questions to ask on their site visit. In a large font, type and print the questions so children may cut their questions out and glue them in their water journals. As partners, students ask their chosen questions and record the responses in their journals. On their return to school, partners report their findings to the class. In a class discussion, recommendations from the children about ways to share (conserve) the water with family and everyone should be recorded on chart paper for students to view. Partners choose one suggestion for sharing to implement at home or at school.

C. Water Everywhere (World Water Wash) (I, G)

Materials: watercolor paints, wax-based crayons, watercolor paper, the book, inflatable primary globes, *The Amazing Pop-up Geography Book*, pictures of ocean animals

In a full-class setting, distribute inflatable globes so that there is at least one for every two students. Focus attention on the amount of blue signifying water that is represented on the globe. Using the globes and *The Amazing Pop-up Geography Book*, conduct a discussion about the composition of our world, especially the percentage of water that is apparent. Talk about the types of animals that live in the oceans and the consequences of not sharing the oceans equally among all nations. Post some pictorial examples for the children. Each student chooses one ocean animal and records the name and a picture of that animal in the water journal. On the watercolor paper, each individual will draw the chosen ocean animal with crayons remembering to press hard enough to leave a good wax base. Once the animal has been completely designed and colored, students dip paintbrushes into water and wash the paper. Next, dip the brush into blue watercolor and wash the paper again. The ocean animal should appear in vivid color. Once the artwork is dry, each child presents the animal and describes why it's important to care for and share them.

The Whispering Cloth: A Refugee's Story

The Connection: *The Whispering Cloth: A Refugee's Story* by Pegi Deitz Shea, 1995

Genre: Historical Fiction, Picture Book

Level: Bridge

Reader: Student

The Book: Refugees can be found in many third-world nations around the globe. The focus of this story was the homeless Hmong people, who because of their beliefs fled their homeland for safety in a refugee camp. Mai and her grandmother were refugees who stitched and sold the traditional embroidered cloth, the pa'ndau, to save money to leave the camp. Having been taught the stitching by her grandmother, Mai made a pa'ndau based on her memories and her dreams. When she was finished, she refused to sell the cloth because it symbolized the story of her family and her dreams.

Human Rights Article(s):

Article 1: Right to equality

Article 2: Freedom from discrimination

Article 3: Right to life, liberty, personal security

Article 13: Right to free movement in and out of the country

NCSS Standard(s):

I. Culture

II. Time, Continuity, and Change

IV. Individual Development and Identity

VI. Power, Authority, and Governance

IX. Global Connections

Knowledge:

- Define refugee.
- Identify and locate various refugee groups around the world including the Hmong.
- Describe the conditions that force children into refugee camps.
- Explain the circumstances in which Mai found herself as a refugee.
- Describe the pa'ndau and its relationship to Hmong culture.

Skills:

- Gather information, using the book and electronic sources, about the causes that result in children becoming refugees and the relief agencies that help them.
- Compare the causes resulting in children becoming refugees among the Hmong with another refugee group.

- Analyze the needs of refugee children around the world based on the information gathered.
- Evaluate the various methods in which the needs of refugee children can be met.
- Create and implement a project that aids refugee children.

Value(s): Children should be free to live and grow in their own homeland.

Activities: I = Individual   P = Partners   G = Group

A. Refugees Around the World (I, G)

Materials: wall map of the world, blank outline map of the world, children's atlas, colored pencils, markers, computer with Internet connection, pushpins, dictionary

Depending on the age of students, individually or as a full group, use Internet sources to identify refugee camps around the world. Second-grade students may need to work with the teacher to locate refugee camps both on the computer on their blank outline maps while third and fourth graders may be able to work individually. Using the Hmong people as an example, label the country names with marker and color the world maps with the source country (Laos) in one color and the refugee camp country (Thailand) in another color. Once as many refugee camps and source countries as possible have been labeled and colored the refugee groups must be identified in a map key. Symbols or numbers chosen for the map key should be placed appropriately on the world maps. Once the maps are completed, children should meet in a full-group setting to share their information. The teacher will place information that has been shared on the wall map using pushpins and labels identifying particular refugee groups. Before asking questions, as a group, determine the definition of "refugee" using the dictionary and any other information collected.

Questions to Ask:
1. How would you describe a refugee?
2. Where can refugees be found in the world, today? What areas seem to have more refugees?
3. What are some of the names of groups who have become refugees?
4. Why do you think so many children have become refugees?
5. What were the conditions that forced Mai to become a refugee?
6. How do you think children in other areas of the world became refugees?

B. Personal Dream Cloth (I)

Materials: muslin fabric cut in 8½ x 14 rectangles, legal-sized copy paper, crayons, pinking shears, fabric paint and crayons in various colors

Children should be requested to think about what they value most in their own lives using Mai's dreams as depicted in her pa'ndau as examples. Using the idea that they could possibly become refugees and be forced to leave behind things they value, individuals must determine what they would most likely want to have with them during their exodus and their time in a refugee camp. Using this dream, individuals will draw and color a model of their stories on the legal-sized paper. Once the model is refined and considered complete, individuals will replicate their dreams onto the muslin rectangles using fabric paints and fabric crayons making their own pa'ndaus. Students share their pa'ndaus and the reasons for choosing their dreams with the class before displaying them in the school.

C. Refugee Relief (G)

Materials: computer with Internet access, collected items as required for project participation

In a group meeting, students and the teacher should discuss the needs of refugee children around the world and determine ways to bring relief to them. Using the Internet, the teacher may facilitate the search for organizations that help refugees. Once a thorough investigation has been conducted, the children should choose a particular refugee group and organization through which to work. During discussions, the children can determine how they could help and the resources they have available or could reasonably obtain to design and implement an assistance plan. If possible, the children should make e-mail contact with children at this particular refugee camp or other camps to find out what needs the children who are refugees may have. The data collected could be used to formulate and carry out the assistance plan. Of course, kid-to-kid contact through e-mail would be significant in terms of a sharing of feelings, frustrations, and hopes as well as a learning experience for the class. Students with teacher help will contact the organization to determine whether the plan is feasible. A finalized plan should become the ongoing, class "service" project with adjustments made as deemed necessary to fulfill the goals of the plan.

CARING CORNER

Moshi Moshi

The Connection: *Moshi Moshi* by Johnathan London, 1998

Genre: Picture Storybook

Level: Bridge

Reader: Teacher & Student

The Book: When a Japanese boy, Kenji, wrote a letter to a class in the United States inviting a student to visit him and become his friend during summer holidays, a young boy and his older brother Elliot found themselves living on Kenji's farm in Japan. A bit reluctant at first, the boy experienced a different culture that included eating eels, practicing Kendo, visiting temples, participating in a tea ceremony, and wearing a kimono and dancing to the drums at a festival. Playing baseball with Kenji seemed to be the activity that strengthened the bond of friendship between the two boys. Back home, the boy realized that though their cultures were dissimilar, there was much similarity between the two boys especially their hope for world peace.

Human Rights Article(s):

Article 27: Right to participate in the cultural life of community

NCSS Standard(s):

I. Culture

IV. Individual Development and Identity

IX. Global Connections

The Amazing Pop-up Geography Book

The Connection: *The Amazing Pop-up Geography Book* by Kate Petty and Jennie Maizels, 2000

Genre: Nonfiction, Information Book

Level: Primary, Bridge

Reader: Teacher & Student

The Book: As there are over six billion people who populate and consume the natural resources of the world, it has become essential that students begin early to know and care about the facets of their home, Earth. The book is chock full of physical and cultural geographical information depicted in colorful and intriguing ways. The students would be involved in a delightful journey of discovery of outer space to inner space. This pop-up, pull-out, push-out, and pull-up book would motivate students' interest in the world around them.

Human Rights Article(s):

Article 3: Right to life, liberty, personal security

NCSS Standard(s):

III. People, Places, and Environments

IX. Global Connections

Cuban Kids

The Connection: *Cuban Kids* by George Ancona, 2000

Genre: Nonfiction, Picture Book

Level: Bridge, Intermediate

Reader: Student

The Book: The author, a noted photojournalist, revisited Cuba, his former homeland, after being away more than forty years. His objective was to ascertain how the children fared under the Communist regime of Fidel Castro. With his camera, he followed individual children and groups of youth at school, work, and play. His colorful photographs depict his findings. Despite living in poor conditions relative to modern, technological nations, the children do get free education, medical care, and recreational services provided by the government. It is apparent that there exists warm, loving care of the children within the family circle. Cuban kids are similar to children in nearby United States and in all other countries.

Human Rights Article(s):

Article 12: Freedom from interference with privacy, family, home and correspondence

Article 13: Right to free movement in and out of the country

Article 25: Right to adequate living standard

Article 27: Right to participate in the cultural life of community

NCSS Standard(s):

I. Culture

II. Time, Continuity and Change

IV. Individuals, Groups, and Institutions

VI. Power, Authority, and Governance

Child of the Warsaw Ghetto

The Connection: *Child of the Warsaw Ghetto* by David A. Adler, 1995

Genre: Historical Fiction

Level: Intermediate

Reader: Student

The Book: The horrible life of Polish Jews in the Warsaw ghetto, from its inception in 1940 to its destruction by Nazis in 1943, was movingly told by a young Jewish boy. Wearing his

Star of David armband, Froim Baum along with some 400,000 were forced to live within an area of seventy-three city streets enclosed by barbed wire. Although death was the punishment for trying to leave, Froim would often take off his band, sneak out to the farmers' market and bring food back to his mother. When the Nazis began to empty the ghetto to send the people to the death camp, Froim's mother got the family smuggled out of the ghetto before their resettlement happened. His freedom lasted a short time before the family was recaptured. Froim was sent to several death camps before being liberated by U.S. soldiers.

Human Rights Article(s):

> Article 2: Freedom from discrimination
> Article 3: Right to life, liberty, personal security
> Article 5: Freedom from torture, degrading treatment
> Article 18: Freedom of belief and religion

NCSS Standard(s):

> I. Culture
> II. Time, Continuity, and Change
> VI. Power, Authority, and Governance

Global Warming:
The Threat of Earth's Changing Climate

The Connection: *Global Warming: The Threat of Earth's Changing Climate* by Laurence Pringle, 2001
Genre: Nonfiction, Chapter Book
Level: Intermediate
Reader: Student
The Book: This information book presents evidence concerning an environmental problem, global warming, that will lead to grave consequences for the people of the world. Industrialized nations are burning fossil fuels that are damaging the ozone that protects the earth from the sun's ultraviolet rays. This results in climatic changes such as the earth getting warmer, widespread drought conditions, and the polar ice cap beginning to melt. The author urged the nations to unite in saving the earth for future generations.

Human Rights Article(s):

> Article 3: Right to life, liberty, and personal security
> Article 25: Right to adequate living standard

NCSS Standard(s):

> III. People, Places, and Environments
> V. Individuals, Groups, and Institutions

VI. Power, Authority, and Governance
VII. Production, Distribution, and Consumption
IX. Global Connections

The Butterfly

The Connection: *The Butterfly* by Patricia Polacco, 2000
Genre: Historical Fiction, Picture Storybook
Level: Bridge, Intermediate
Reader: Teacher & Student
The Book: During the Nazi occupation of France, many brave people hid Jews in their homes until safe passage out of the country could be arranged. Monique formed a friendship with Severine, a Jewish girl who spent her days with her parents hiding in Monique's basement. Meeting only at night, Monique would bring objects from the outside for Severine to experience, such as a butterfly. Both were spotted at the window as they released a butterfly. Monique, her mother, and Severine escaped undetected from the house and traveled during the night to get Severine to a safe point. As a parting gift Monique gave a pet cat to her friend. Back in their home garden, weeks later, dozens of butterflies fluttered around Monique and her mother. The girl knew it was a sign that Severine was safe.

Human Rights Article(s):

Article 2: Freedom from discrimination
Article 3: Right to life, liberty, personal security
Article 9: Freedom from arbitrary arrest, exile
Article 13: Right to free movement in and out of the country
Article 18: Freedom of belief and religion

NCSS Standard(s):

III. Time, Continuity, and Change
V. Individuals, Groups, and Institutions
VI. Power, Authority, and Governance

One Boy from Kosovo

The Connection: *One Boy from Kosovo* by Trish Marx, 2000
Genre: Nonfiction, Picture Book
Level: Intermediate
Reader: Teacher & Student

The Book: This book chronicles the stay of twelve-year old Edmond Fejzullah, Edi, in the Brazda refugee camp in Macedonia. Edi, an ethnic Albanian living in Kosovo when the Serbian government began a practice of ethnic cleansing, was forced with his family to leave his country. The journey was harrowing with fears that Serbian soldiers would torture or kill those who were not Serbs. The border crossing was especially dangerous. When Edi and his family reached the refugee camp at Brazda, life changed drastically. Instead of living in a large two-story house, he now shared a tent with his family as well as his Aunt Sanye and her family. For two months, Edi slept in crowded conditions, played in dust and mud, stood in lines for water, food, and other necessities, and dreamed of going home. This books provides an accounting of Edi's experiences during his stay in the refugee camp before returning home at the war's end.

Human Rights Article(s):

Article 2: Freedom from discrimination
Article 3: Right to life, liberty, personal security
Article 5: Freedom from torture, degrading treatment
Article 25: Right to adequate living standard
Article 26: Right to education

NCSS Standard(s):

  I. Culture
  II. Individuals, Groups, and Institutions
  VI. Power, Authority, and Governance
  IX. Global Connections

Chi-Hoon: A Korean Girl

The Connection: *Chi-Hoon: A Korean Girl* by Patricia McMahon, 1993
Genre: Nonfiction, Picture Book
Level: Bridge
Reader: Teacher & Student
The Book: Kim Chi-hoon lived with her parents and older sister, Kim Chi-young, in an apartment in Yoido, Korea. The book relates a week of activities in the life of Chi-hoon accompanied by her brief, nightly, diary entries (school children are required to keep diaries). On Monday morning, Chi-hoon was at the weekly school assembly where she again failed to win a class prize. The girl decided that by being extra kind and helpful to others, especially her sister, she would win. The text and photographs not only provided a look at her efforts but also her work and play at home and school including foods she ate, her trip to the temple, her visit with grandparents, and the tennis and piano lessons. Despite her good works, Chi-hoon always remained hopeful that she might succeed in her quest.

Human Rights Article(s):

    Article 24: Right to rest and leisure

    Article 26: Right to an education

    Article 27: Right to participate in the cultural life of the community

NCSS Standard(s):

    I. Culture

    IV. Individual Development and Identity

Hostage to War

The Connection: *Hostage to War: A True Story* by Tatjana Wassiljewa, 1997

        Genre: Nonfiction, Chapter Book

        Level: Intermediate

       Reader: Student

       The Book: A true story written about a young Russian girl concerning the inhumane effects of war and captivity for all people particularly children. Tatjana's happy family life was interrupted when the Nazis invaded Russia in 1941. She was taken away from her parents to Germany as a captive laborer to work long hours in a factory as well as a farm camp. The girl was constantly hungry, exhausted, and despondent over the loss of her freedom and schooling. When the war ended Tatjana returned to discover that life was not much better at home. Her determination and hope made her struggle for an education that resulted in her becoming a teacher.

Human Rights Article(s):

    Article 3: Right to life, liberty, personal security

    Article 5: Freedom from torture, degrading treatment

    Article 12: Freedom from interference with privacy, family, home and correspondence

    Article 13: Right to free movement in and out of the country

    Article 26: Right to education

NCSS Standard(s):

    II. Time, Continuity, and Change

    IV. Individual Development and Identity

    VI. Power, Authority, and Governance

Extraordinary Girls

The Connection: *Extraordinary Girls* by Maya Ajmera, Olateju Omolodun, and Sarah Strunk, 1999

Genre: Nonfiction, Chapter Book

Level: Intermediate

Reader: Student

The Book: The authors' objective was to celebrate girlhood around the world. In this effort, she was most successful. It was evident from the text and the rich, beautifully colored photographs that despite their different national and cultural backgrounds, there was a commonality among the girls. There existed in their behaviors and resultant actions a similarity in their courage, perseverance, creativity, peace-seeking efforts, talents, joy of games and sport, belief in the importance of education, and compassion and caring for others. An example of this was the girl who cared deeply about foster children who moved from family to family carrying their belongs in garbage bags that she organized the Suitcases for Kids movements. Girls are truly extraordinary individuals who can make a difference.

Human Rights Article(s):

Article 1: Right to equality

Article 3: Right to life, liberty, personal security

Article 26: Right to education

Article 29: Community duties essential to free and full development

NCSS Standard(s):

I. Culture

IV. Individual Development and Identity

IX. Global Connections

Polar, the Titanic Bear

The Connection: *Polar, the Titanic Bear* by Daisy Corning Stone Spedden, 1994

Genre: Picture Storybook

Level: Bridge, Intermediate

Reader: Teacher & Student

The Book: Polar, a very special toy bear, was a parting gift to Master, the only son of wealthy Daisy and Frederick Spedden. Through the beady eyes of Polar, who accompanied his master everywhere, the life of the very affluent is detailed. Traveling to many countries by liner, rail, and auto, boy and bear experienced the best that money could provide including tickets on the *Titanic*. Able to leave the sinking ship by lifeboat, the Speddens and Polar survived the bitter cold night. When all humans were rescued, Polar was left behind until saved by a seaman. The two friends had a joyful reunion. The Speddens spent the rest of the voyage caring for the other less fortunate survivors.

Human Rights Article(s)

      Article 3: Right to life, liberty, personal security

      Article 29: Community duties essential to free and full development

NCSS Standards(s):

    I. Culture

    II. Time, Continuity, and Change

    X. Civic Ideals and Practices

Wake Up World! A Day in the Life of Children around the World

The Connection: *Wake Up World! A Day in the Life of Children around the World* by Beatrice Hollyer, 1999

Genre: Picture Storybook

Level: Primary, Bridge

Reader: Teacher & Student

The Book: To become a caring member of the global community, students need to be able to identify and empathize with children in near and distant lands. The students' sense of identification and empathy could come about through knowledge and understanding of the similarities, yet uniqueness, in lifestyles among children in the world. The text and photos in the book could foster this understanding. During one day, it follows eight children from different cultures who were involved in activities that are common to all children such as waking up, getting dressed, going to school, doing home tasks, eating, and sharing dreams.

Human Rights Article(s):

      Article 29: Community duties essential to free and full development

NCSS Standard(s):

    I. Culture

    II. Individual Development and Identity

    IX. Global Connections

Sadako and the Thousand Paper Cranes

The Connection: *Sadako and the Thousand Paper Cranes* by Eleanor Coerr, 1999
Genre: Historical Fiction, Chapter Book
Level: Intermediate
Reader: Student
The Book: Sadako a vibrant young girl, who lived in Hiroshima when the atom bomb was dropped, could run like the wind. She practiced religiously for her school race. Everyone remarked about her dedication and ability. As she was racing she began to notice dizziness, but rather than alarm her parents she kept it to herself. Eventually, Sadako found herself in the hospital desperately ill with the atom bomb disease, leukemia. Her best friend, Chizuko, while visiting her in the hospital, brought a golden crane and told her the story of the crane and its ability to live for a thousand years. In the hope of the gods granting her wish and making her healthy, Sadako folded 644 origami cranes before she died. One thousand paper cranes were buried with her after her classmates folded the rest as a tribute to her courage.

Human Rights Article(s):

    Article 3: Right to life, liberty, personal security
    Article 5: Freedom from torture, degrading treatment
    Article 18: Freedom of belief and religion

NCSS Standard(s):

    I. Culture
    II. Time, Continuity, and Change
    IV. Individual Development and Identity
    VI. Power, Authority, and Governance

This book is particularly helpful in teaching children empathy and ways to take positive social action. There are many websites dedicated to Sadako with activities in which children may engage.

http://www.sadako.org

http://www.sadako.com

http://asterix.ednt.lsu.edu/~edtech/webquest/sadako.htm

The Little Ships: The Heroic Rescue at Dunkirk in World War II

The Connection: *The Little Ships: The Heroic Rescue at Dunkirk in World War II* by Louise Borden, 1997.
Genre: Historical Fiction, Picture Storybook
Level: Intermediate
Reader: Student

The Book: On the beaches of Dunkirk in May 1940, a half million British and French soldiers were trapped between the German soldiers and the English Channel. When the call came for small ships to rescue the men, hundreds of small fishing boats manned by civilians joined the ships of the Royal Navy to form an armada of 861 vessels on this caring mission. The harrowing nine days that these boats were ferrying soldiers from the beaches to the large troop carriers is told through the eyes of young girl who accompanied her father on their boat, *The Lucy*. She worked tirelessly helping soldiers board the boat, baling water, and bringing solace to the wounded. Despite the strafing by a dive bomber on their last run *The Lucy* made safe port in England.

Human Rights Article(s):
> Article 3:   Right to life, liberty, personal security
> Article 13:   Right to free movement in and out of the country

NCSS Standard(s):
> II. Time, Continuity, and Change
> V. Individuals, Groups, and Institutions
> VI. Power, Authority, and Governance
> X. Civic Ideals and Practices

Baseball in the Barrios

The Connection: *Baseball in the Barrios* by Henry Horenstein, 1997
Genre: Nonfiction, Picture Book
Level: Intermediate
Reader: Student
The Book: Hubaldo, a fifth grader, told about baseball, *béisbal*, as it is played in the neighborhoods, the barrios, throughout Venezuela. There are organized leagues for various age levels with appropriate uniforms and equipment. Although Hubaldo plays in the Infantels league, his love of the sport finds him using all his free time to play pick-up games on a variety of surfaces with materials that could be adapted as equipment. Rolled-up socks have been used as balls while wooden planks have made useful bats. Hubaldo and other boys in the barrio care for the game and follow their heroes who play in the Venezuelan professional leagues. As baseball is enjoyed by players and spectators in both North and South America, it has become a hemispheric connector and a true all-American game.

Human Rights Article(s):
> Article 24:   Right to rest and leisure
> Article 25:   Right to adequate living standard
> Article 27:   Right to participate in the cultural life of community

NCSS Standard(s):
  I. Culture
  IV. Individual Development and Identity
  IX Global Connections

CARING COLLECTION: WORLD

Adler, D. A. (1995). *Child of the Warsaw Ghetto*. New York: Holiday House.

Ajmera, M., O. Omolodun, & S. Strunk. (1999). *Extraordinary Girls*. Watertown, MA: Charlesbridge Publishing.

Ancona, G. (2000). *Cuban Kids*. New York: Marshall Cavendish.

Bang, M. (1997). *Common Ground: The Water, Earth, and Air We Share*. New York: The Blue Sky Press.

Borden, L. (1997). *The Little Ships: The Heroic Rescue at Dunkirk in World War II*. New York: Margaret K. McElderry Books.

Coerr, E. (1997). *Sadako and the Thousand Paper Cranes*. New York: Puffin Books.

Hollyer, B. (1999). *Wake up, World! A Day in the Life of Children Around the World*. New York: Henry Holt.

Horenstein, H. (1997). *Baseball in the Barrios*. San Diego, CA: Gulliver Books.

Laufer, P. (2000). *Made in Mexico*. Washington, DC: National Geographic Society.

London, J. (1998). *Moshi Moshi*. Brookfield, CT: The Millbrook Press.

Marx, T. (2000). *One Boy from Kosovo*. New York: HarperCollins Publishers.

McMahon, P. (1993). *Chi-hoon: A Korean Girl*. Honesdale, PA: Boyds Mills Press.

Polacco, P. (2000). *The Butterfly*. New York: Philomel Books.

Pringle, L. (2001). *Global Warming: The Threat of the Earth's Changing Climate*. New York: Seastar Books.

Rubin, S. G. (2000). *Fireflies in the Dark: The Story of Freidl Dicker-Brandeis and the Children of Terezin*. New York: Holiday House.

Schrier, J. (1998). *On the Wings of Eagles*. Brookfield, CT: The Millbrook Press.

Shea, P. D. (1995). *The Whispering Cloth: A Refugee's Story*. Honesdale, PA: Boyds Mills Press.

Sisulu, E. B. (1996). *The Day Gogo Went to Vote*. Boston: Little, Brown.

Spedden, D. C. (1997). *Polar, the Titanic Bear*. Boston: Little, Brown.

Wassiljewa, T. (1999). *Hostage to War: A True Story*. New York: Scholastic.

Appendix A
Curriculum Standards for Social Studies

Ten Thematic Strands in Social Studies

Social studies programs should include experiences that provide for the study of the folowing:

I. **Culture.** Social studies programs should include experiences that provide for the study of *culture and cultural diversity*.

II. **Time, Continuity, and Change.** Social studies programs should include experiences that provide for the *ways human beings view themselves in and over time*.

III. **People, Places, and Environments.** Social studies programs should include experiences that provide for the study of *people, places, and environments*.

IV. **Individual Development and Identity.** Social studies programs should include experiences that provide for the study of *individual development and identity*.

V. **Individuals, Groups, and Institutions.** Social studies programs should include experiences that provide for the study of *interactions among individuals, groups, and institutions*.

VI. **Power, Authority, and Governance.** Social studies programs should include experiences that provide for the study of *how people create and change structures of power, authority, and governance*.

VII. **Production, Distribution, and Consumption.** Social studies programs should include experiences that provide for the study of *how people organize for the production, distribution, and consumption of goods and services*.

VIII. **Science, Technology, and Society.** Social studies programs should include experiences that provide for the study of *relationships among science, technology, and society*.

IX. **Global Connections.** Social studies programs should include experiences that provide for the study of *global connections and interdependence*.

X. **Civic Ideals and Practices.** Social studies programs should include experiences that provide for the study of *the ideals, principles, and practices of citizenship in a democratic republic*.

Appendix B
Universal Declaration of Human Rights
(Abbreviated)

Student Resource Sheet

Now, therefore THE GENERAL ASSEMBLY proclaims this Universal Declaration of Human Rights as a common standard of achievement for all peoples and all nations, to the end that every individual and every organ of society, keeping this Declaration constantly in mind, shall strive by teaching and education to promote respect for these rights and freedoms:

Article 1	Right to equality
Article 2	Freedom from discrimination
Article 3	Right to life, liberty, personal security
Article 4	Freedom from slavery
Article 5	Freedom from torture, degrading treatment
Article 6	Right to recognition as a person before the law
Article 7	Right to equality before the law
Article 8	Right to remedy by competent tribunal
Article 9	Freedom from arbitrary arrest, exile
Article 10	Right to a fair public hearing
Article 11	Right to be considered innocent until proven guilty
Article 12	Freedom from interference with privacy, family, home and correspondence
Article 13	Right to free movement in and out of the country
Article 14	Right to asylum in other countries from persecution
Article 15	Right to a nationality and freedom to change it
Article 16	Right to marriage and family
Article 17	Right to own property
Article 18	Freedom of belief and religion
Article 19	Freedom of opinion and information
Article 20	Right of peaceful assembly and association
Article 21	Right to participate in government and in free elections

Article 22 Right to social security

Article 23 Right to desirable work and to join trade unions

Article 24 Right to rest and leisure

Article 25 Right to adequate living standard

Article 26 Right to education

Article 27 Right to participate in the cultural life of community

Article 28 Right to social order assuring human rights

Article 29 Community duties essential to free and full development

Article 30 Freedom from state or personal interference in the above rights

(Source: University of Minnesota Human Rights Resource Center. *Universal Declaration of Human Rights* [Abbreviated]. [n.d.] Retrieved June 27, 2002, from http://www.hrusa.org.)

Appendix C
I-BE-IT Model

I-BE-IT Model

Pre-reflection

Identification

Reflection

Bracketing

Empathy

Post-reflection

Insight

Transference

GUIDELINES FOR CONDUCTING I-BE-IT

Pre-Reflection

Identification

List all of the characteristics about the protagonist that could be matched with characteristics of students today (age, gender, family, location, abode, chores, interests, recreation, friends, problems, hopes).

Reflection

Bracketing

To initiate and stimulate the mental imagery, set the spatial boundaries, and describe where the action takes place noting climate, dress, interrelationship of the people within the spatial boundaries, and the ways people are or are not caring about each other.

Empathy

Read a brief selection relating to the protagonist and the action in the event. Students empathize (share) the same feelings that the character is feeling (fear, anxiety, homesickness, jealousy, happiness, anger, hate) within that lived experience.

Post-Reflection

Insight

The students interpret the significance of feelings that are related to the occurrences of humanness in the lived experience of the character. Ask students questions about the actions the character took and the reasons for taking them. How would it feel to take the same action? Note the consequences of the humane actions that result within that lived experience. Insight occurs when students can make judgments about the true nature of the event in relation to themselves and to others.

Transference

Connect the feelings about being humane that were aroused and resulted from this sharing the lived experience with the book character to the attitudes and actions in today's world.

For example, how can you follow the character's actions by being humane in your own life? What actions can you set in place to demonstrate caring behaviors?

Paradigm of the Lived Experience Using Literature

Bud, Not Buddy by Christopher Paul Curtis
Protagonist: Bud Caldwell

Pre-Reflection

Preparing Students and Environment

1. Students are seated in a comfortable fashion.
2. Only a sheet of paper and a pen are on the students' desks.
3. Students are seated in desks that are facing forward preferably toward a barren wall; this is so they will not be distracted or able to make eye contact with other students.
4. They should be prepared to cover and close eyes when directed by the teacher.

Identification

Teacher talks with the students about the book and the character, Bud Caldwell. Students are to think about how they are alike. There are several ways in which Bud is like the students in this class. He is a ten year old who has his own rules for living. He lives in a city and loves to visit the library. He saves his favorite things and guards them carefully. He's very curious about the activities that go on around him. If you put modern clothes on the character that youngster could walk into the classroom and be very much like the students who are there today. If we had a time machine, it could carry us back to the historical time in which the character lived. How very nice to have a personal time machine — our minds to take this journey back in time, we need to be able to concentrate. Shutting eyes and covering them with hands helps the process to occur. Keep in mind all the things that we have identified as being similar between Bud and you.

Reflection

Bracketing

Close your eyes and concentrate on shutting out everything that is today and picture yourself 65 years ago in the same setting in which Bud Caldwell once lived. Imagine the city of Flint, Michigan where many poor and ragamuffin children live in orphanages or foster homes. Bud has lost his mother and is on a desperate search for his father. He has just ran away from an abusive foster home where he beat up the cruel, 12-year old son of his foster parents and was locked in an outdoor shed overnight. He found his friend, Bugs, and together they begin looking for Hooperville to hop a train and get to the West to find work so they wouldn't be hungry anymore. Once he enters the cardboard city south of Flint, Bud surveys the scene. For as far as he can see there are raggedy huts, people of all colors, mostly men, sitting together, and only a few women and children. Everyone is desperate and hungry and worried about the future, just like him. Bud has found "Hooverville."

Empathy

Now, you are Bud Caldwell. Put yourself in his place. Look through his eyes. Experience what he experiences. Feel what he feels. What do you see? What does this scene do to you? How does it make you feel? — When you first see the desperate people living in appalling conditions, what do you think? — When you become aware that they are all hungry and fearful? — When you realize that Hooperville is really Hooverville and it exists many times over throughout the country; there so many others trying to find a future? — When you know you will have to ask for food from hungry people? — How do you feel when you are welcomed to join them? — What did you feel when you are asked to pitch in and help?

[Open your eyes. Pick up your pencils and write a description of the lived moment and share those with the class.]

Post-Reflection

Insight

What caring action did Bud take? Why did he take it? In Bud's place, would you have done the same thing? Why? How does it feel to take the same action? Why did he continue to search for a better life? What were the consequences of his caring actions in this caring scenario? During this time period, many people were out of work, desperate, and hungry. Most communities failed to have the services to help those in need, How do you think this affected the lives of children?

Transference

What are some ways in which your community helps children and adults who are hungry? How could you help those in need?

Paradigm of the
Lived Experience Using Literature

The Story of Ruby Bridges by Robert Coles
Protagonist: Ruby Bridges

Pre-Reflection

Preparing Students and Environment

5. Students are seated in a comfortable fashion.
6. Only a sheet of paper and a pen are on the students' desks.
7. Students are seated in desks that are facing forward preferably toward a barren wall; this is so they will not be distracted nor able to make eye contact with other students.
8. They should be prepared to cover and close eyes when directed by the teacher.

Identification

Teacher talks with the students about the book and the character, Ruby Bridges. Students are to think about how they are alike. There are several ways in which Ruby is like the students in this class. She is attends an elementary school, lives with her parents and a brother and sister in a city. She goes to school and caries her books and a lunch box. She's very curious about the activities that go on around her. If you put modern clothes on the character that youngster could walk into the classroom and be very much like the students who are there. If we had a time machine, it could carry us back to the historical time in which the character lived. How very nice to have a personal time machine—our minds! To take this journey back in time, we need to be able to concentrate. Shutting eyes and covering them with hands helps the process to occur. Keep in mind all the things that we have identified as being similar between Ruby and yourself.

Reflection

Bracketing

Close your eyes and concentrate on shutting out everything that is today and picture yourself forty-one years ago in the same setting in which Ruby Bridges once lived. Imagine the large city of New Orleans where black children and white children attend separate schools. Ruby is the first black child to attend William Frantz Elementary School. Federal marshals carrying guns are assigned to safeguard six-year-old Ruby as she enters the school. An angry crowd is lined up in front of the building. They yell terrible things, carry signs that say they don't want her there. This event repeats itself everyday for months. Once she enters the building there are no other children present, only Mrs. Henry, her teacher. She is the sole student in this classroom day after day. The angry mob greets Ruby as she leaves school as well. Ruby hurries through the crowd without saying a word. She feels sorry for them and prays twice a day so that God would forgive them for their terrible actions.

Empathy

Now, you are Ruby Bridges. Put yourself in her place. Look through her eyes. Experience what she experiences. Feel what she feels. What do you see? What does this scene do to you? How does it make you fee?—When you first see the angry mob lined up in front of school?—When you become aware that they are yelling awful things at you, carrying signs that tell you to go home?—When you notice that the school is empty; there are no other students?—When it's time to go home and the furious people are there again?—How do you feel when you pray for them?—What did you feel when you got home?

[Open your eyes. Pick up your pencils and write a description of the lived moment and share those with the class.]

Post-Reflection

Insight

What caring action did Ruby take? Why did she take it? In Ruby's place, would you have done the same thing? Why? How does it feel to take the same action? Why did she continue to return to the Frantz Elementary School day after day? What were the consequences of her caring actions in this caring scenario? During this time period, many people held prejudices against blacks. Most schools, especially in the South, were segregated. How do you think this affected the lives of children both white and black?

Transference

What are some ways in which you could act more like Ruby? How could you help others feel welcomed into your school? How can you insure that unfair situations don't happen at your school? What actions could you take to change those situations?

Bibliography

MY SELF

Aliki. (1984). *Feelings*. New York: HarperCollins Publishers.

Armstrong, W. H. (1989). *Sounder*. New York: HarperCollins Juvenile Books.

Beatty, P. (1989). *Charley Skedaddle*. Mahwah, NJ: Troll.

Blackwood, G. (1998). *The Shakespeare Stealer*. New York: Puffin Books.

Bruchac, J. (1998). *A Boy Called Slow*. New York: The Putnam & Grosset Group.

Clark, M. G. (1991). *Freedom Crossing*. New York: Scholastic Paperbacks.

Creel, A. H. (1999). *A Ceiling of Stars*. Middletown, WI: Pleasant Company Publications.

Curtis, J. L. (1998). *Today I Feel Silly & Other Moods That Make My Day*. New York: HarperCollins Publishers.

Cushman, K. (1995). *The Midwife's Apprentice*. New York: HarperCollins Publishers.

dePaola, T. (1996). *The Baby Sister*. New York: Penguin Putnam Books for Young Readers.

Edwards, J. A. (1999). *Little Bo: The Story of Bonnie Boadicea*. New York: Hyperion Books for Children.

Fenner, C. (1991). *Randall's Wall*. New York: Aladdin Paperbacks.

Freymann, S., and J. Elffers. (1999). *How Are You Peeling? Foods with Moods*. New York: Scholastic Press.

Haddix, M. P. (1997). *Running out of Time*. New York: Aladdin Paperbacks.

Hissey, J. (1986). *Old Bear*. New York: Philomel Books.

Hissey, J. (1999). *Little Bear's Trousers*. New York: Philomel Books.

Hood, S. (1999). *Bad Hair Day*. New York: The Putnam & Grosset Group.

Johnson, D. B. (2000). *Henry Hikes to Fitchburg*. Boston: Houghton Mifflin.

Kilborne, S. S. (1994). *Peach & Blue*. New York: Alfred A. Knopf.

Lee, J. M. (1991). *Silent Lotus*. New York: Farrar, Straus & Giroux.

Nicleodhas, S. (1989). *Always Room for One More*. New York: Henry Holt.

London, J. (1997). *Ali Child of the Desert*. New York: Lothrop, Lee, & Shepard Books.

Lucado, M. (1997). *You Are Special*. Wheaton, IL: Crossway Books.

Mandelbaum, P. (1993). *You Be Me, I'll Be You*. New York: Kane/Miller Book Publishers.

Martin, J. B. (1998). *Snowflake Bentley*. Boston: Houghton Mifflin.

McCully, E. A. (1992). *Mirette on the High Wire.* New York: G. P. Putnam's Sons.

McDonald, M. (2000). *Judy Moody.* Cambridge, MA: Candlewick Press.

McKissack, P. C. (2000). *The Honest-to-Goodness Truth.* New York: Atheneum Books for Young Readers.

Minters, F. (1997). *Cinder-Elly.* New York: Puffin Books.

Mitchell, L. (1999). *Different Just Like Me.* Watertown, MA: Charlesbridge Publishing.

Mora, F. X. (1991). *The Tiger and the Rabbit: A Puerto Rican Folktale.* Chicago: Children's Press.

Morrison, T., and S. Morrison. (1999). *The Big Box.* New York: Hyperion Books for Children.

Osborne, M. P. (2000). *Adaline Falling Star.* New York: Scholastic.

Pfister, M. (2001). *Milo and the Mysterious Island.* New York: North-South Books.

Pfister, M. (1992). *The Rainbow Fish.* New York: North-South Books.

Pinkney, B. (1997). *Max Found Two Sticks.* New York: Aladdin Paperbacks.

Robertson, B. (1999). *Marguerite Makes a Book.* Los Angeles: J. Paul Getty Museum.

Rogers, F. (2001). *Let's Talk About It: Extraordinary Friends.* New York: G. P. Putnam's Sons.

San Souci, R. D. (1989). *The Talking Eggs.* New York: Dial Books for Young Readers.

Shannon, D. (1998). *A Bad Case of Stripes.* New York: The Blue Sky Press.

Sheindlin, J. (2000). *Win or Lose by How You Choose!* New York: Cliff Street Books.

Simon, C. (1999). *I Like to Win!* Brookfield, CT: The Millbrook Press.

Steig, W. (1988). *Brave Irene.* New York: Farrar, Straus & Giroux.

Trent, J. (1993). *There's a Duck in My Closet.* Dallas: Word Publishing.

Vaughan, M. (1999). *Abbie Against the Storm: The True Story of a Young Heroine and a Lighthouse.* Hillsboro, OR: Beyond Words Publishing, Inc.

Wallace, B. (1994). *The Biggest Klutz in the Fifth Grade.* New York: Minstrel Books.

MY FAMILY

Adler, D. A. (1993). *A Picture Book of Anne Frank.* New York: Holiday House.

Blume, J. (1991). *Tales of a Fourth Grade Nothing.* New York: Bantam Doubleday Dell Books for Young Readers.

Breathed, B. (2000). *Edwurd Fudwupper Fibbed Big.* Boston: Little, Brown.

Breckler, R. (1996). *Sweet Dried Apples.* Boston: Houghton Mifflin.

Brink, C. R. (1993). *Baby Island.* New York: Aladdin Paperbacks.

Brodkin, A. M. (1998). *The Lonely Only Dog.* New York: Scholastic.

Carlson, N. S. (1990). *The Family Under the Bridge.* New York: Harper & Row Junior Books.

Catalanotto, P. (1999). *Dad and Me.* New York: DK Publishing.

Couloumbis, A. (2000). *Getting Near to Baby.* New York: Putnam Publishing Group.

Curtis, C. P. (1999). *Bud, Not Buddy.* New York: Delacorte Press.

Curtis, G. (1998). *The Bat Boy and His Violin.* New York: Simon & Schuster Books for Young Readers.

dePaola, T. (1999). *26 Fairmount Avenue*. New York: G. P. Putnam's Sons.

Garza, C. L. (1999). *Magic Windows/Ventanas Mágicas*. San Francisco: Children's Book Press.

———. (1991). *A Piece of My Heart/Pedacito de Mi Corazón*. New York: The New Press.

Gilman, P. (1992). *Something from Nothing*. New York: Scholastic.

Goble, P. (1989). *Beyond the Ridge*. New York: Simon & Schuster.

Greenberg, K. (1994). *Family Abuse: Why Do People Hurt Each Other*. New York: Twenty-First Century Books.

Guback, G. (1994). *Luka's Quilt*. New York: Greenwillow Books.

Haas, J. (2000). *Hurry!* New York: Greenwillow Books.

Haughton, E. (2000). *Rainy Day*. Minneapolis, MN: Carolrhoda Books.

Kiuchi, T. (1993). *The Lotus Seed*. San Diego: Harcourt Brace.

Kroll, V. (1993). *A Carp for Kimiko*. Watertown, MA: Charlesbridge Publishing.

Love, D. A. (1995). *Bess's Log Cabin Quilt*. New York: Bantam Doubleday Dell Books for Young Readers.

Martin, J. B. (2001). *The Lamp, the Ice, and the Boat Called Fish*. New York: Houghton Mifflin.

Mathers, P. (1995). *Kisses from Rosa*. New York: Alfred A. Knopf.

Monk, I. (1999). *Hope*. Minneapolis, MN: Carolrhoda Books.

Onyefulu, I. (1998). *Grandfather's Work: A Traditional Healer in Nigeria*. Brookfield, CT: The Millbrook Press.

Patterson, K. (1987). *The Great Gilly Hopkins*. New York: HarperTrophy.

Peacock, C. A. (2000). *Mommy, Far, Mommy Near: An Adoption Story*. Morton Grove, IL: Albert Whitman.

Polacco, P. (1999). *Luba and the Wren*. New York: Penguin Putnam Books for Young Readers.

Reeder, C. (1991). *Shades of Gray*. New York: Avon Books.

Rosenberg, L. (1999). *The Silence in the Mountains*. New York: Orchard Books.

Salinas, B. (1998). *The Three Pigs/Los Tres Cerdos*. Alameda, CA: Piñata Publications.

Schaefer, C. L. (2000). *The Copper Tin Cup*. Cambridge, MA: Candlewick Press.

Smucker, B. (1999). *Selina and the Bear Paw Quilt*. New York: Dragonfly Books.

Soros, B. (1998). *Grandmother's Song*. New York: Barefoot Books.

Steptoe, J., illustrator. (1997). *In Daddy's Arms I Am Tall: African Americans Celebrating Fathers*. New York: Lee & Low Books.

Stewart, S. (2001). *The Journey*. New York: Farrar, Straus & Giroux.

Tax, M. (1996). *Families*. New York: The Feminist Press.

White, K. (2000). *When They Fight*. Delray Beach, FL: Winslow Press.

Wickham, M. (1996). *A Golden Age*. Washington, DC: The Smithsonian Institution.

Wright, B. R. (1991). *The Scariest Night*. New York: Scholastic.

Wyeth, S. D. (1995). *Always My Dad*. New York: Scholastic.

Yep, L. (1990). *Dragonwings*. New York: Scholastic.

OUR SCHOOL

Allard, H. (1988). *Miss Nelson Has a Field Day*. Boston: Houghton Mifflin.

Beneduce, A. K. (2000). *Philipok*. New York: Philomel Books.

Clements, A. (1997). *Double Trouble in Walla Walla*. Brookfield, CT: The Millbrook Press.

———. (2000). *The Janitor's Boy*. New York: Simon & Schuster.

Coles, R. (1995). *The Story of Ruby Bridges*. New York: Scholastic.

Couric, K. (2000). *The Brand New Kid*. New York: Doubleday.

Coville, B. (1999). *There's an Alien in My Backpack*. New York: Pocket Books.

Day, L. (1999). *Rockett's World: Are We There Yet?* New York: Scholastic.

DeClements, B. (1990). *Nothing's Fair in Fifth Grade*. New York: Puffin Books.

dePaola, T. (2001). *Meet the Barkers: Morgan & Moffat Go to School*. New York: Putnam Publishing Group.

Duffey, B. (1995). *How to Be Cool in the Third Grade*. New York: Puffin Books.

Gorman, C. (1999). *Dork in Disguise*. New York: HarperCollins Publishers.

Henkes, K. (1996). *Lilly's Purple Plastic Purse*. New York: Greenwillow Books.

Jiménez, F. (1998). *La Mariposa*. Boston: Houghton Mifflin.

Kline, S. (1997). *Horrible Harry in Room 2B*. New York: Puffin Books.

Levine, M. (2000). *Keeping a Head in School: A Student's Book About Learning Abilities and Learning Disorders*. Cambridge, MA: Educators Publishing Service.

Martin, A. (1993). *Rachel Parker, Kindergarten Show-off*. New York: Holiday House.

McDonald, M. (2000). *Judy Moody*. Cambridge, MA: Candlewick Press.

Rowling, J. K. (1999). *Harry Potter and the Sorcerer's Stone*. New York: Scholastic.

Say, A. (1995). *Stranger in the Mirror*. Boston: Houghton Mifflin.

Shannon, D. (1999). *David Goes to School*. New York: The Blue Sky Press.

Slate, J. (2000). *Miss Bindergarten Stays Home from Kindergarten*. New York: Dutton Children's Books.

Strasser, T. (1996). *Help! I'm Trapped in My Gym Teacher's Body*. New York: Scholastic.

Surat, M. (1999). *Angel Child, Dragon Child*. New York: Econo-Clad Books.

Tolstoy, L., retold by A. Keay. (2000). *Philipok*. New York: Philomel Books.

Wallace, B. (1992). *The Biggest Klutz in Fifth Grade*. New York: Pocket Books.

OUR NEIGHBORHOOD

Adler, D. A. (1995). *Child of the Warsaw Ghetto*. New York: Holiday House.

Bash, B. (1996). *In the Heart of the Village: The World of the Indian Banyan Tree*. San Francisco: Sierra Club Books for Children.

Brumbeau, J. (2000). *The Quiltmaker's Gift*. Duluth, MN: Pfeifer-Hamilton Publishers.

Bruchac, J. (1998). *The Arrow Over the Door*. New York: Dial Books for Young Readers.

Bunting, E. (1994). *Smoky Night*. San Diego: Harcourt Brace.

Burton, V. L. (1999). *The Little House*. Boston: Houghton Mifflin.

Christiansen, C. (1997). *The Mitten Tree*. Golden, CO: Fulcrum Publishing.

Collier, B. (2000). *Uptown*. New York: Henry Holt.

Cushman, K. (1996). *The Ballad of Lucy Whipple*. New York: HarperTrophy.

Demi. (1997). *One Grain of Rice*. New York: Scholastic Press.

DiSalvo-Ryan, D. (2001). *Grandpa's Corner Store*. New York: HarperCollins.

Fix, P. (1994). *Not So Very Long Ago: Life in a Small Country Village*. New York: Dutton Children's Books.

Hartas, L. (1995). *The Apartment Book*. New York: Dorling Kindersley Publishing.

Horenstein, H. (1997). *Baseball in the Barrios*. San Diego: Gulliver Books.

Howe, J. (1997). *Pinky and Rex and the New Neighbors*. New York: Aladdin Paperbacks.

Irwin, H. (1979). *The Lilith Summer*. New York: The Feminist Press.

Jenness, A. (1993). *Come Home with Me: A Multicultural Treasure Hunt*. The New Press.

Krensky, S. (1989). *Witch Hunt: It Happened in Salem Village*. New York: Random House

Lester, H. (1999). *Tacky the Penguin*. Boston: Houghton Mifflin.

Merriam, E. (2000). *On My Street*. New York: HarperCollins.

Moss, M. (2001). *Emma's Journal*. San Diego: Harcourt Brace & Company.

Raskin, E. (1966). *Nothing Ever Happens on My Block*. New York: Aladdin Books.

Ringgold, F. (1991). *Tar Beach*. New York: Crown Publishers.

Sandburg, C. (1999). *The Huckabuck Family*. New York: Farrar, Straus & Giroux.

Smith, C. L. (2001). *Jingle Dancer*. New York: HarperCollins.

Soto, G. (1992). *Pacific Crossing*. New York: Harcourt Brace.

Wegman, W. (1998). *My Town*. New York: Hyperion Books for Children.

Wheatley, N. (1992). *My Place*. Brooklyn, NY: Kane/Miller Book Publishers.

Yolen, J. (1998). *Raising Yoder's Barn*. Boston: Little, Brown.

Zolotow, C. (1989). *The Hating Book*. New York: Harper Trophy.

OUR NATION

Adler, D. A. (1990). *A Picture Book of George Washington*. New York: Holiday House.

———. (2000). *America's Champion Swimmer: Gertrude Ederle*. San Diego: Gulliver Books.

Altman, L. J. (2000). *The Legend of Freedom Hill*. New York: Lee & Low Books.

Amstel, M. (2000). *Sybil Ludington's Midnight Ride*. Minneapolis: Carolrhoda Books.

Bailer, D. (1997). *Wanted—A Few Bold Riders: The Story of the Pony Express*. Washington, DC: The Smithsonian.

Bartoletti, S. C. (1999). *Kids on Strike!* Boston: Houghton Mifflin.

Bates, K. L. (1993). *America the Beautiful*. New York: Atheneum Books for Young Readers.

Borden, L. W. (1999). *A. Lincoln and Me*. New York: Scholastic Press.

Brandt, K. (1993). *Rosa Parks: Fight for Freedom.* Mahwah, NJ: Troll

Brodsky, J. (1999). *Discovery.* New York: Farrar, Straus & Giroux.

Broyles, A. (2000). *Shy Mama's Halloween.* Gardiner, ME: Tilbury House Publishers.

Bruchac, J. (2000). *Crazy Horse's Vision.* New York: Lee & Low Books.

———. (2000). *Sacajawea.* San Diego: Silver Whistle.

———. (2000). *Squanto's Journey: The Story of the First Thanksgiving.* San Diego: Silver Whistle.

Carter, A., and C. Saller. (2000). *George Washington Carver.* Minneapolis, MN. Carolrhoda Books.

Cary, B. (1989). *Meet Abraham Lincoln.* New York: Random House.

Cooney, B. (1996). *Eleanor.* New York: Viking Press.

Curry, B. K., and J. M. Brodie. (1996). *Sweet Words So Brave: The Story of African American Literature.* Madison, WI: Zino Press Children's Books.

Denenberg, B. (1997). *So Far from Home: The Diary of Mary Driscoll, an Irish Mill Girl.* New York: Scholastic.

Fritz, J. (1997). *Bully for You, Teddy Roosevelt!* New York: Penguin Putnam Books for Young Readers.

———. (1998). *Who's That Stepping on Plymouth Rock?* New York: The Putnam & Grosset Group.

Gauch, P. L. (1994). *Thunder at Gettysburg.* New York: Young Yearling.

Guthrie, W. (1998). *This Land Is Your Land.* Boston: Little, Brown.

Hermes, P. (2001). *Our Strange New Land: Elizabeth's Journey.* New York: Scholastic.

Himler, R. (1995). *Nettie's Trip South.* New York: Scholastic.

Hopkins, D. (1995). *Sweet Clara and the Freedom Quilt.* New York: Random House.

Hunt, I. (1986). *Across Five Aprils.* New York: Penguin Putnam.

Johnston, T. (1996). *The Wagon.* New York: William Morrow.

Keller, L. (1998). *The Scrambled States of America.* New York: Henry Holt.

King, W. (2001). *Children of the Emancipation.* Minneapolis, MN: Carolrhoda Books.

Lasky, K. (1998). *Dreams in the Golden Country: The Diary of Zipporah Feldman, a Jewish Immigrant Girl.* New York: Scholastic.

Lawrence, J. (1993). *The Great Migration: The American Story.* New York: HarperCollins Children's Books.

Lester, J. (1998). *From Slave Ship to Freedom Road.* New York: Puffin Books.

——— (1988). *To Be a Slave.* New York: Scholastic.

Loomis, C. (2000). *Across America, I Love You.* New York: Hyperion Books for Children.

McCully, E. A. (1996). *The Bobbin Girl.* New York: Dial Books for Young Readers.

Mochizuki, K. (1993). *Baseball Saved Us.* New York: Lee & Low Books.

Moss, M. (1999). *Emma's Journal: The Story of a Colonial Girl.* Orlando, FL: Harcourt Brace.

——— (1998). *Rachel's Journal: The Story of a Pioneer Girl.* Orlando, FL: Harcourt Brace.

Ringgold, F. (1995). *My Dream of Martin Luther King.* New York: Crown Publishers.

——— (1992). *Underground Railroad in the Sky.* New York: Crown Publishers.

Rockwell, A. (2000). *Only Passing Through: The Story of Sojourner Truth.* New York: Alfred A. Knopf.

Ryan, P. M. (1996). *The Flag We Love.* Watertown, MA: Charlesbridge Publishing.

Sandler, M. W. (1995). *Immigrants.* New York: HarperCollins Publishers.

San Souci, R. D. (1993). *Cut from the Same Cloth: American Women of Myth, Legend, and Tall Tale.* New York: Puffin Books.

St. Gorge, J. (2000). *So You Want to Be President?* New York: Philomel Books.

Schanzer, R. (2000). *Escaping to America: A True Story.* New York: HarperCollins Publishers.

Stewart, S. (2001). *The Journey.* New York: Farrar, Straus & Giroux.

Stux, E. (2001). *Writing for Freedom: A Story about Lydia Maria Child.* Minneapolis, MN: Carolrhoda Books.

West, D. C., and J. M. West. (2001). *Uncle Sam and Old Glory: Symbols of America.* New York: Antheneum for Young Readers.

Williams, S. A. (1997). *Working Cotton.* San Diego: Harcourt Brace Jovanovich.

Zeifert, H. (1998). *When I First Came to This Land.* New York: G. P. Putnam's Son.

OUR WORLD

Adler, D. A. (1995). *Child of the Warsaw Ghetto.* New York: Holiday House.

Ajmera, M., O. Omolodun, and S. Strunk. (1999). *Extraordinary Girls.* Watertown, MA: Charlesbridge Publishing.

Ancona, G. (2000). *Cuban Kids.* New York: Marshall Cavendish.

Atkins, J. (1995). *Aani and the Tree Huggers.* New York: Lee & Low Books.

Bang, M. (1997). *Common Ground: The Water, Earth, and Air We Share.* New York: Scholastic.

Bial, R. (1996). *With Needle and Thread: A Book about Quilts.* Boston: Houghton Mifflin.

Blanco, A. (1994). *Angel's Kite/La Estrella de Angel.* Children's Book Press.

Borden, L. (1997). *The Little Ships: The Heroic Rescue at Dunkirk in World War II.* New York: Margaret K. McElderry Books.

Breckler, R. (1996). *Sweet Dried Apples.* Boston: Houghton Mifflin.

Brewster, H. (1996). *Anastasia's Album.* New York: Hyperion Books for Children.

Brown, A., and A. Langley. (1999). *What I Believe: A Young Person's Guide to the Religions of the World.* Brookfield, CT: The Brookfield Press.

Cha, D. (1996). *Dia's Story Cloth.* New York: Lee & Low Books.

Coerr, E. (1999). *Sadako and the Thousand Paper Cranes.* New York: Puffin Books.

Deitz, P. (1995). *The Whispering Cloth.* Honesdale, PA: Boyds Mills Press.

Delacre, L. (1993). *Vejigante Masquerader.* New York: Scholastic.

Durell, A., and M. Sachs, eds. (1990). *The Big Book for Peace.* New York: Dutton Children's Books.

Freedman, R. (1993). *Eleanor Roosevelt: A Life of Discovery.* New York: Clarion Books.

Heide, F. P., and J. H. Gilliland. (1995). *Sami and the Time of the Troubles.* New York: Clarion Books.

Hollyer, B. (1995). *Stories from the Classical Ballet.* New York: Viking Press.

———. (1999). *Wake Up, World! A Day in the Life of Children Around the World.* New York: Henry Holt.

Horenstein, H. (1997). *Baseball in the Barrios*. San Diego, CA: Gulliver Books.

Huynah, Q. N. (1997). *Water Buffalo Days: Growing up in Vietnam*. New York: HarperCollins Juvenile Books.

Innocenti, R. (1999). *Rose Blanche*. Mankato, MN: Creative Editions.

Jiang, J. L. (1997). *Red Scarf Girl: A Memoir of the Cultural Revolution*. New York: HarperTrophy.

Kindersley, B., and A. Kindersley. (1995). *Children Just Like Me: A Unique Celebration of Children Around the World*. New York: Dorling Kindersley Publishing.

———. (1997). *Children Just Like Me: Celebrations*. New York: Dorling Kindersley Publishing.

Knight, M. B., and M. Melnicove. (2001). *Africa Is Not a Country*. Brookfield: CT: The Millbrook Press.

Laufer, P. (2000). *Made in Mexico*. Washington, DC: National Geographic Society.

Le Tord, B. (1995). *A Blue Butterfly: A Story about Claude Monet*. New York: Delacorte Press.

London, J. (1997). *Ali, Child of the Desert*. New York: Lothrop, Lee & Shepard Books.

———. (1998). *Moshi Moshi*. Brookfield, CT: The Millbrook Press.

Marx, T. (2000). *One Boy from Kosovo*. New York: HarperCollins Publishers.

Maruki, T. (1982). *Hiroshima No Pika*. New York: William Morrow.

McMahon, P. (1993). *Chi-hoon: A Korean Girl*. Honesdale, PA: Boyds Mills Press.

———. (1997). *Six Words, Many Turtles and Three Days in Hong Kong*. Boston: Houghton Mifflin.

Mercredi, M. (1997). *Fort Chipewyan Homecoming: A Journey to Native Canada*. Minneapolis, MN: Lerner Publication Company.

Miles, B. (1991). *Save the Earth: An Action Handbook for Kids*. New York: Alfred A. Knopf.

Mullins, P. (1994). *V for Vanishing: An Alphabet of Endangered Animals*. New York: HarperCollins Publishers.

Nhuong, H. Q. (1997). *Water Buffalo Days: Growing Up in Vietnam*. New York: Harper Trophy.

Olaleye, I. (1998). *Lake of the Big Snake*. Honesdale, PA: Boyds Mills Press.

Petty, K., and J. Maizels. (2000). *The Amazing Pop-up Geography Book*. New York: Dutton Children's Books.

Polacco, P. (2000). *The Butterfly*. New York: Philomel Books.

Presilla, M., and G. Soto. (1996). *Life Around the Lake: Embroideries by the Women of Lake Patzcuaro*. New York: Henry Holt.

Pringle, L. (2001). *Global Warming: The Threat of Earth's Changing Climate*. New York: SeaStar Books.

———. (1993). *Jackal Woman: Exploring the World of Jackals*. New York: Scribner.

Rose, D. L. (1990). *The People Who Hugged the Trees*. Niwot, CO: Roberts Rinehart, Inc. Publishers.

Rubin, S. G. (2000). *Fireflies in the Dark: The Story of Freidl Dicker-Brandeis and the Children of Terezin*. New York: Holiday House.

Say, A. (1993). *Grandfather's Journey*. Boston: Houghton Mifflin.

Schrier, J. (1998). *On the Wings of Eagles: An Ethiopian Boy's Story*. Brookfield, CT: The Millbrook Press.

Schur, M. R. (1994). *Day of Delight: A Jewish Sabbath in Ethiopia*. New York: Dial Books for Young Readers.

Shea, P. D. (1995). *The Whispering Cloth: A Refugee's Story*. Honesdale, PA: Boyds Mills Press.

Sisulu, E. B. (1996). *The Day Gogo Went to Vote: South Africa, April 1994*. Boston: Little, Brown.

Sorensen, H. (2000). *The Yellow Star: The Legend of King Christian X of Denmark*. Atlanta, GA: Peachtree Books.

Spier, P. (1988). *People*. New York: Doubleday.

Spedden, D. C. (1997). *Polar, the Titanic Bear*. Boston: Little, Brown.

Strom, Y. (1993). *Uncertain Roads: Searching for the Gypsies*. New York: Four Winds Press.

Tolstoy, L., retold by A. K. Beneduce. (2000). *Philipok*. New York: Philomel Books.

Wartski, M. C. (1980). *A Boat to Nowhere*. New York: Penguin Books.

Wassiljewa, T. (1999). *Hostage to War: A True Story*. New York: Scholastic.

Wheatley, N., and D. Rawlins. (1994). *My Place*. Brooklyn, NY: Kane/Miller Book Publishers.

World Book Encyclopedia. (1998). *Stand Up for Your Rights*. Chicago: World Book.

OTHER REFERENCES

Benard, B. (1993). Fostering resiliency in kids. *Educational Leadership, 51*(3), 44–48.

Elias, M. J., J. E. Zins., et al. (1997). *Promoting social and emotional learning: Guidelines for educators*. Alexandria, VA: Association for Supervision and Curriculum Development.

Freeman, E. B., and D. G. Person. (1998). *Connecting informational children's books with content area learning*. Needham Heights, MA: Allyn & Bacon.

Krey, D. M. (1998). *Children's literature in social studies: Teaching to the standards*. Washington, DC: National Council for the Social Studies.

National Council for the Social Studies. (1994). *Expectations of excellence: Curriculum standards for social studies*. Washington, DC.

Peter, L. J. (1979). *Peter's Quotations: Ideas for Our Time*. New York: William Morrow and Co., Inc.

Rocha, R., and O. Roth. (1995). *The universal declaration of human rights: An adaptation for children*. New York: United Nations Publications.

United Nations Department of Public Information. (1998). *Universal Declaration of Human Rights*. New York.

University of Minnesota Human Rights Resource Center. *Universal Declaration of Human Rights* (Abbreviated). (n.d.) Retrieved June 27, 2002, from http://www.hrusa.org.

Index